Folk Lullabies of the World

Seventy-seven traditional folk lullabies from every corner of the globe

Compiled and edited by
Barbara and Michael Cass-Beggs

Oak Publications
London/New York/Paris/Sydney/Copenhagen/Berlin/Madrid/Tokyo

TRANSLATIONS AND ACKNOWLEDGEMENTS

Lullabies should be sung in their original language, but since this is not always possible, English translations have been provided. Where translations were not already available, the authors have enlisted the help of many friends, who were able to provide literal and accurate translations. These translations were not designed to fit the music, and in adapting them the author has tried as far as possible to retain the literal meaning of the words.

The authors would like to express their thanks to the following, for translations of the songs, and in many cases, further information about them: Danish: Kari Williams, Ottawa; Dutch: Tjok George, Kingston; Jan Kuypers, Toronto; French: Charlotte Jones, Montreal; Gaelic: Major C. I. N. Macleod, Dept. of Celtic Studies, St. Francis Xavier University, Antigonish, Nova Scotia; German: Nadair Woroby, Regina; Hungarian: Maria Trebuss, Regina; Icelandic: Dr. H. Bessance and Mrs. H. Skerlassan, Dept. of Icelandic Literature, University of Manitoba, Winnipeg; Indian: T. R. Anand, Montreal; Israeli: Valerie Sloman, Montreal; Maltese: Louis Grech, Ottawa; Polish: Nadair Woroby, Regina; Portuguese: Valerie Sloman, Montreal; Portuguese Dialect: Portuguese Embassy, Ottawa; Sinhalese: Mrs. L. S. B. Perera, wife of the High Commissioner for Ceylon, Ottawa; Spanish: Charlotte Jones, Montreal; Lillian Mendelssohn, who had already translated some of the lullabies collected by her and used in this book.

PHOTOGRAPHS

Philip Gendreau: Pages 10, 12, 14, 16, 18, 27, 29, 32, 35, 36, 47, 49, 51, 53, 59, 62, 65, 79, 83, 87, 91, 93, 96, 99, 102, 109, 110, 112, 113, and 123
David Gahr: Pages 9, 20, 21, 24, 44, 50, 57, 67, and 70
Lee Sherman: Pages 23, 38, and 41
Ray Flerlage: Pages 31 and 76
Julius Lester: Page 107
Milly Wise: Page 121

Cover design by Studio Twenty, London
Computer management by Adam Hay Editorial Design
Original text design by Jean Hammons

This book © Copyright 1969 & 1993 by Oak Publications
A Division of Embassy Music Corporation, New York, NY.

Order No.OK64981
ISBN 0-7119-3470-3

*Exclusive Distributors:*Music Sales Limited
8/9 Frith Street, London W1V 5TZ, England.
Music Sales Corporation *225 Park Avenue South,*
New York, NY10003, USA.
Music Sales Pty Limited*120 Rothschild Avenue,*
Rosebery, NSW 2018, Australia.

Printed in the United Kingdom by
Redwood Books Limited, Trowbridge, Wiltshire.

Contents

Remembering those who sang lullabies to me:

My mother, Caroline Evelyn Maud Cass
My childhood Nanny and very dear friend,
"Bea" Beatrice Crosby Arnold

Dedicated to my younger daughter, Carolyn Ruth Coombs

The Lullaby

It is not surprising that in the story of mankind the mother and child hold a special place, because although father and mother create the child, it is usually the love and care of the mother that keep it alive, and thus keep the race alive.

Naturally the primary part of this love and care is the attention given to the physical needs of the child, but this is not sufficient in itself. Something further is required if the child's well-being is to be maintained: an expression of love. One simple way of expressing this love can be found in the lullaby.

Lullabies are fundamental to our folk cultures. Mothers of every race and country have sung lullabies, made up by themselves, answering the needs of their own particular baby.

Like all folk songs they have been handed down by word of mouth from family to family and have travelled from country to country. In travelling they have changed and developed, and have been sung and listened to by a far larger audience than the audience of one, for whom the song was originally intended.

In primitive days it was understood that a baby needed soft sounds and rhythmic movements to help it to sleep and give it a sense of security. With the development of the sophisticated and hygienic society of Western Europe and North America, lullabies fell into disrepute and were outlawed as old-fashioned or even harmful! Now, the trend has reversed; we accept the fact that the baby needs music, rhythmic sounds and harmonious movement, and we are turning again to the cradles and lullabies of our grandparents.

What are the characteristics of a lullaby? A lullaby is a song sung in love to an audience of one; it is simple, soothing, rhythmic, and repetitive. It is the feeling, and not the words (if there are words) that matters. Although lullabies express joy, happiness and contentment, anxious and unhappy undertones are often present, for mothers are often anxious and unhappy. All serve the purpose, the one purpose of lulling the little one to sleep.

In earlier days, hands could not be spared for the unproductive labor of merely putting a baby to sleep, so cradles were made so that they could be rocked easily with the foot. Where the cradle was not used, for example, in Japan, the baby was slung on its mother's back, where it moved with the rhythm of her work but did not interfere with it!

Lullabies, however simple, are colored by the thoughts, beliefs and feelings of the nation or race from which they come. They also illustrate many different attitudes to the child. Some promise rewards if he will only go to sleep, some promise punishment if he stays awake! All convey the hope that mothers the world over cherish for their babies, the hope that they will be good, brave, happy and secure. It is certainly safe to assume that almost all lullabies originated with the peasant and working woman, who not only sang them to her own babies, but when uprooted and removed from her village or tribe to attend to the children of the wealthy, sang these same lullabies to them. In singing these lullabies, so rich in their own primitive myth and melody, the mother could dream of her own home and baby and find some release from her sorrow and heartache. In reviewing any collection of lullabies one can distinguish between those which primarily concern the mother, although ostensibly sung to the baby, and those sung by the happy and secure mother or mother substitute which affirm the rightness and security of the world and are sung directly for the baby.

Although the rhythm of the lullaby is all important, the language of the lullaby, which is usually onomatopoeic, is colorful and varied since it is the language of diminutives. In addition to the sounds and titles so familiar to all of us, such as lully, lullow, lulla, lo, la, lu, lay, hushabye, rockabye, lullabye, balu lu low, there are the Roman lalla and the Latin loquor and lullare, the Greek nenia, the Spanish nana and the Italian ninne-nanne, the

French dodo and the Israeli eyla. In the Czech language three different words are used to denote sleep: hajej, hynej and dadej.

Lullaby language is a study in itself, as every country has its own language, which is not easy to translate. The difficulty arises from the fact that many of the words used in a lullaby are what is technically known as "baby-talk." For example, the word "lo lo" in a French lullaby has nothing to do with the French for lullaby: it is French baby-talk for "milk." It belongs with "gee-gees" and "beddy-byes"! Baby-talk is a ritual part of the mother and child heritage, and is essential in the Dandling and Play songs which precede the lullaby. When lullabies were rejected, baby-talk too was regarded as unscientific and probably harmful, but without it bed-putting became a somewhat self-conscious and sterile operation. In throwing out the lullaby language with the lullaby, out went "baby, cradle and all"!

It is interesting to take a look at the earliest lullaby terms in common use in England, where the lullaby has been a recognized literary form for at least six centuries, with a folk tradition existing long before that. *Lulla,* as used in carol lullabies, seems to be the earliest and best known term with *lollai* noted in an Anglo-Irish song of thirteen hundred and fifteen and *lullay* in a MS of thirteen hundred and seventy two. *Bye,* meaning sleep, dates back to the fifteenth century. *Hush* is found in the sixteenth century while *hushaby,* as such, is not found in use before the seventeenth century.

The origin and scholarly pursuit of the lullaby is not the concern of those who sing them. They are concerned with their practical application, as an answer to present needs, and as a source of pleasure to themselves and the baby! This is perhaps the reason why lullabies have received very little attention and have been dismissed, much as folk songs were, as musically unimportant, and the sole prerogative of mothers! In actual fact lullabies present us with some of the most simple and beautiful melodies in the world which can be enjoyed by everyone. Certainly mothers sing them, but so do fathers, and they belong equally to maids of all work, nurses, nannies, big sisters and grannies. Sometimes these mother substitutes sing them more often and more lovingly because it is their job to sing them, because they have the time, or perhaps because they have not had the joy of bearing and possessing this baby which is their precious responsibility for so short a time.

Love is limitless, and lullabies belong to all who love babies!

NORTH AMERICAN INDIAN MUSIC

Although there are specific songs and dances which belong to one or other of the Indian tribes, they are all characteristic of North American Indian music. The songs are short, monophonic, and use only a few words, repeated over and over. Their concept of accompaniment is that of doubling the vocal line with primitive wind instruments, and providing a rhythmic background with rattles, sticks, drums, etc. No one is trained as a professional musician, but he does have informal specialization, which is likely to be related to his position in the tribe.

The music is functional, in the sense that it is used as part of other non-musical activities such as story-telling, love-making, fighting, ridiculing, and as an indispensable part of their religious ceremonies; it is valued in terms of what is "good" rather than what is "beautiful." It is thought to possess magic power, because through music one can communicate with, and gain strength from, the power which is behind and part of Nature. Women take part in the musical life of the tribe but their special concern is story-telling, lullabies, and the women's dances. Indian songs are not well-known outside the Indian community, but they have a deep significance within it.

AFRO-AMERICAN SONGS

The Negroes came as slaves from Africa to America, and as they had always sung, danced and drummed as they worked, this habit did not change.

According to Gilbert Chase in *America's Music,* the desire to sing while working was the major impulse for the growth of the Afro-American folksongs, which, as work songs, dance songs, love songs, lullabies, and a variety of other songs, continued to be part of their plantation life.

The spirituals, which are usually emphasized as the main source of Negro music, were actually a later development, and were not a significant part of their culture until the latter part of the eighteenth century, when Negroes were taught and became better acquainted with the white man's religion. The words and images of the evangelical hymns and psalms were then adopted by the Negroes and related to concrete situations in their own environment and experience. The resulting spirituals were sung during work and formed part of the vocal work pattern, as well as being sung in church and at camp meetings.

Just as the white man's religion affected the music of the Negroes, so during certain periods their songs were influenced by the white man's songs. This, according to Newman I. White in his book, *American Negro Folk Songs,* was between 1830 and 1836, when "Jim Crow" Rice and his contemporaries were making the minstrel song popular, and again in the eighteen-nineties, when "coon" and ragtime songs were the popular vogue. In each case, the Negro, who had contributed only slightly to the songs sung about him, adopted the product, changed it in the usual folk manner, and transmitted the changed song to a new generation of his own.

THE BRITISH ISLES

The British Isles boasts an incredible variety of landscapes, dialects and definite local characteristics within a relatively tiny area, and the folk cultures are similarly distinct and interesting. There is the sometimes rather matter-of-fact English folksong and the elaborate music of the Welsh bards, the rhythmic pattern of the Scottish song, and the almost unearthly beauty of a Hebridean folksong, with the curving melody rising and falling to the feel of the sea. Unhappily the two Hebridean lullabies in this book give little idea of the wealth and beauty of the folk-music from these remote Isles, and so faced with a less known culture and imperfect examples, it is perhaps appropriate to give the following more detailed mention of Hebridean folksongs.

SCANDINAVIAN LULLABIES

The Scandinavians have systematically collected their folk songs so that they are now easily available and in daily use. They are rich and varied in character, particularly the Norwegian folk songs, and it is interesting to note that in these lullabies there is no sense of fear or anxiety, only a confident and matter-of-fact pleasure in baby and all that pertains to him. They are light-hearted and convey a sense of contentment and satisfaction.

GERMAN FOLK MUSIC

Germany's music, both folk and composed, has had a great influence on European music, and we are already familiar with many of the folk tunes because they have been used in the music of Mozart, Beethoven, Schubert, Brahms, etc. In Central Europe people were closer to each other and musical ideas, and folk music travelled to and fro. Another feature of the German and Austrian folk music was that it was not confined to one particular group in society but grew up and existed alongside the cultivated and composed music.

CENTRAL AND SOUTH AMERICAN AND WEST INDIAN LULLABIES

These lullabies have a vitality and a richness of rhythm which one would expect from a vital people who have assimilated many different races and cultures. They express an intimacy and often a passion which is entirely lacking in the European and Western lullabies. Attention is focused on mother and baby now, rather than in the future, and they convey the sense of hardship which mothers endure to keep their little ones safe and happy.

EGYPTIAN AND NIGERIAN LULLABIES

Ancient Egypt had a rich musical culture but, alas, little is left to tell its story, apart from what was preserved in Turkey and its influence on Greek music. Luckily many examples of musical instruments and music-making can be seen in Egyptian paintings and sculpture. Egyptian folk music is Arabic in style with its trills, elaborate decorations and scale formation. Today Egypt is regarded as the cultural centre of the Arab world.

Nigerian music is not simple music to play or understand. It abounds in complicated rhythms which are played on the drums and a variety of other percussion instruments. The drum beats constitute a language in themselves, in addition to being used as an accompaniment to their songs.

From babyhood children listen to the drums and absorb their rhythms, and this process is further helped by the father who will touch and move the baby in response to the rhythmic patterns. Thus, at a very early age children acquire an advanced degree of rhythmical response, and when the time comes for them to play the drums they already know most of their complicated language. There are at least three different types of "talking drums," all of which can be made to give a wide variety of notes.

INDIAN AND SINHALESE LULLABIES

Indian music constitutes one of the world's most complex and sophisticated musical cultures with its "ragas," highly organized melodies and scale systems, and its "tala" system, an orderly study of countless rhythmic forms. It is not surprising therefore that the better known lullabies reflect elaborate and beautifully organized melodies, which need the native instruments and Indian voice to do them justice.

The rhythm of the Sinhalese lullaby is patterned on the swaying or rocking motion of a "sari" in which the baby is placed, with one end of it fastened to the rafters of the house. The other end is pulled gently by the singer of the chant or lullaby. The lullaby is called a chant as even if the melody differs from chant to chant, the rhythm remains the same and this allows the singer to sing many different word versions to one chant.

Lullabies are rarely sung by the mother, for if she is a peasant woman she is out at work in the fields with her husband, and if she is a wealthy woman, a nurse would attend to the needs of her baby. The chants are therefore sung by an older sister, a younger sister of the mother of the baby, or more often they are sung by the grandmother.

JEWISH LULLABIES

Only one of these lullabies comes directly from Israel; the others are from Eastern Europe. It is difficult, however, to classify songs which emerge from such a variety of countries and backgrounds, and yet spring from the same people, and this variety is intensified when one considers the songs of the Oriental and Spaniolic Jews. The secular folksongs are mainly in the Yiddish vernacular, but a small number are in archaic Yiddish, and as such they go back to the sixteenth century in Western Europe.

Up to World War II, the largest Jewish community was based in Germany. Since then America and Israel have provided a home and absorbed the greatest number of Jewish people.

Naturally some of the oldest songs are lullabies, and these, like all lullabies, reflect the basic aspirations of the race. The mother's first choice is always that her son may become a scholar and a God-fearing man, and if scholarship is out of the question because of financial difficulties, then her second choice is that her son become a good business man, but still remain a pious and God-fearing man. If the Israeli lullaby included here is characteristic of the new lullabies, then they too echo in a large measure the melodic feeling and ideas of the previous century.

Most of these lullabies have a number of verses, so there is time to reflect upon and describe to the baby both current happenings and the story of his race. Throughout there is an undercurrent of sadness and suppressed struggle, yet they are full of hope for the small son to whom they are sung.

No lullabies seem to be directly composed for the girl baby, who is only mentioned in terms of a future wife, or someone who at an early age will sing lullabies to her small brother. The mother lives through her son, for it is he who gives the family prestige, and in this aspect the lullabies reflect the patriarchal nature of the society and the importance attached to the continuance of the race.

Canada

Ba Ba Baby — *Micmac Indian*
Dors Dors Le P'tit Bibi — *Acadian*
Tah Ne Bah — *Souix Indian*
Bí Bí Og Blaka — *Icelandic*
Still Now And Hear My Singing — *Eskimo*
C'est La Poulette Grise — *French-Canadian*
Ho Ho Watanay — *Iroquois Indian*

Ba Ba Baby

Collected by Dr. Helen Creighton in the Maritimes, this lullaby was sung by Miss Denny of Eels Ground, New Brunswick. The words sung to the lullaby are just crooning sounds and need no translation. *Micmac Indian*

Ba ba bidu bidu ba,
Ba ba baby, bidju bidju.
Baby bidju ba ba bidju ba.

Dors Dors Le P'tit Bibi

SLEEP SLEEP LITTLE BABY

The French who settled in the Maritime Provinces were called Acadians. This lullaby was collected by Dr. Helen Creighton in Pubuico, the oldest of the Acadian villages. It was sung by Mrs. Laure Irene McNeil. *Acadian*

Dors, dors le p'tit bibi,
C'est le beau p'tit bibi à mama.
Dors, dors, dors, dors,
Dors, dors, le bibi à mama.
Demain s'y fait beau,
J'irons au grand père,
Dors, dors, le p'tit bibi.
Dors, dors, dors, dors,
Dors le beau p'tit bibi à mama.

Sleep, sleep little baby,
You're such a lovely Mother's little one.
Sleep, sleep, sleep, sleep,
Sleep, sleep, Mother's baby.
Tomorrow if it's fine,
We will see Grand-pa.
Sleep, sleep little baby.
Sleep, sleep, sleep, sleep,
Sleep my love, Mother's little baby.

Tah Ne Bah

GO TO SLEEP

This lullaby was sung to the author by Mrs. Dorothy Francis of Regina, Saskatchewan, who had learnt it from her grandmother, a Saulteaux Indian. Although of Indian origin, the song has obviously been influenced by western music. The Sioux and Saulteaux tribes are both Plains Indians, and the term Saulteaux applies to Sioux Indians who come from the Sault Ste. Marie area. *Sioux Indian*

Tah ne bah, ne chan e aiz,
Ne chan e aiz, ne chan e aiz.
Tah ne bah se,
Chan e aiz, chan e aiz.
Tah ne bah, chan e aiz.

Go to sleep my little one,
My little baby, my little one.
Go to sleep now,
Little one, little one.
Go to sleep, little one.

Bí Bí Og Blaka

BYE BYE AND HUSH NOW

This well-known and much loved lullaby is sung by Icelandic families in Canada. It employs the rather clever device of insisting that the baby stay awake in order to hear the swans sing as they fly (for their singing is supposed to sound like tinkling bells). The effort involved in trying to stay awake promptly sends the baby to sleep! Where the words refer to baby thinking of "little lambs at play" one assumes that in adult terms this means "counting sheep." *Icelandic*

Bí bí og blaka,
Álftirnar kvaka.
Ég laet sem ég sofi,
En samt mun ég vaka.
Bíum bíum bamba,
Börnin litlu pamba.
Fram á fjallá kamba
Pau fará ad leita lamba.

By by and hush now,
Can you see the swans fly?
You may pretend to go to sleep,
But I know you will want to peep.
Bíum bíum bamba, sleep little baby,
You'll fall asleep when your thoughts stray
To little lambs at play.

Still Now And Hear My Singing

The Rev. D. H. Whitbread, an Anglican missionary who worked among the Eskimos of Port Harrison, Quebec, collected this song, which comes from Cape Dorset on the southern coast of Baffinland. He composed the words which are a free interpretation of the Eskimo verses.   *Eskimo*

Still now and hear my sing - ing, Sleep through the night, my Dar - ling.

We have a ti - ny daugh - ter, Thanks be to God who sent her.

Still now and hear my singing,
Sleep through the night, my Darling.
We have a tiny daughter,
Thanks be to God who sent her.

Though she as yet knows nothing,
She is so sweet I'm singing.
We have a tiny daughter,
Thanks be to God who sent her.

C'est La Poulette Grise

THE GREY HEN

Here is one of the best known and best loved of the French folk lullabies that is very well known in French Canada. The English translation given here is by Alan Mills. Any number of verses can be sung depending on the versatility of the singer and the sleepiness of the baby! *French-Canadian*

C'est la pou-let-te gri-se Qui pond dans l'é-gli-se Ell' va pon-dre un pe-tit co-co Pour son p'tit qui va fair do-di-che, Ell' va pon-dre un pe-tit co-co Pour son p'tit qui va fair do-do. Do-di-che Do-do.

There is a grey hen ba-by, In the church my ba-by, She will lay a pret-ty lit-tle egg Just for you if you go to sleep now, She will lay a pret-ty lit-tle egg Just for you if you go to sleep. Sleep now my ba-by.

C'est la poulette grise	*There is a grey hen baby,*
Qui pond dans l'église,	*In the church my baby,*
Ell' va pondre un petit coco	*She will lay a pretty little egg*
Pour son p'tit qui va fair dodiche	*Just for you if you go to sleep now,*
Ell' va pondre un petit coco	*She will lay a pretty little egg*
Pour son p'tit qui va fair dodo	*Just for you if you go to sleep*
Dodiche, dodo.	*Sleep now my baby.*
C'est la poulette brune	*There is a brown hen baby*
Qui pond dans la lune.	*In the moon my baby*
C'est la poulette blanche	*There is a white hen baby*
Qui pond dans les branches.	*In the branch my baby*

Ho Ho Watanay

SLEEP SLEEP LITTLE ONE

This lullaby comes from one of the most important of Canada's Indian tribes. It was collected by Alan Mills from the Caughnawaugha Indian Reservation near Montreal in 1955. The majority of the Canadian Iroquois live in the province of Ontario, but there are many Iroquois Indians living in the U.S.A.
Iroquois Indian

Ho, ho, wa-ta-nay,
Ho, ho, wa-ta-nay,
Ho, ho, wa-ta-nay,
Ki-yo-ke-na, ki-yo-ke-na.

Sleep, sleep, little one,
Sleep, sleep, little one,
Sleep, sleep, little one,
Now go to sleep, now go to sleep.

18

United States

All The Pretty Little Horses — *Appalachians, Virginia*
O Mother Glasco — *Afro-American*
Mary Had A Baby — *Afro-American*
Bye Bye Baby — *Appalachians, Virginia*
The Mocking Bird — *Appalachians, Virginia*

All The Pretty Little Horses

This version of the lullaby was collected by Moe Asch and is similar to one collected by Cecil Sharp called *Mammy Loves.* Other words heard more frequently in the southern states are given below, and are probably closer to the original words sung by the Negro mammy as she attends to the little white baby in her care and worries about her own little baby.

"Hushaby don't you cry,
Go to sleepy little baby
Way down yonder in the medder
There's a poor little lambie,
The bees and the butterflies
Peckin' out his eyes,
The poor little lamb cries Mammy." *Appalachian*

Rhythmically

Hush - a - bye, don't you cry, Go to sleep, lit-tle ba - by.

When you wake, you shall take, All the pret-ty lit-tle hors - es;

Blacks and bays, dap-ples and grays, Coach and six lit-tle hors - es.

Hush - a - bye, don't you cry, Go to sleep, lit-tle ba - by.

Hushaby, don't you cry,
Go to sleep, little baby.
When you wake, you shall take
All the pretty little horses;
Blacks and bays, dapples and grays,
Coach and six little horses.
Hushaby, don't you cry,
Go to sleep, little baby.

O Mother Glasco

This lullaby is similar in content and thinking to *All the Pretty Little Horses* and may well be another version of the same lullaby. *Afro-American*

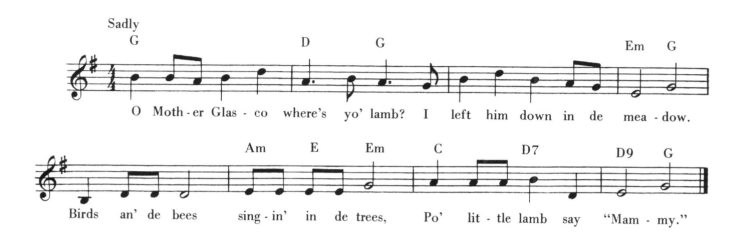

O Moth-er Glas-co where's yo' lamb? I left him down in de mea-dow.

Birds an' de bees sing-in' in de trees, Po' lit-tle lamb say "Mam-my."

O Mother Glasco where's yo' lamb?
I left him down in de medder.
Birds and de bees, singin' in de trees,
Po' little lamb say "Mammy."

Mary Had A Baby

This is a Christmas spiritual rather than a lullaby. On the other hand its very definite rhythm and the extemporaneous character of its verses suggest its use and justifies its inclusion as a lullaby. *Afro-American*

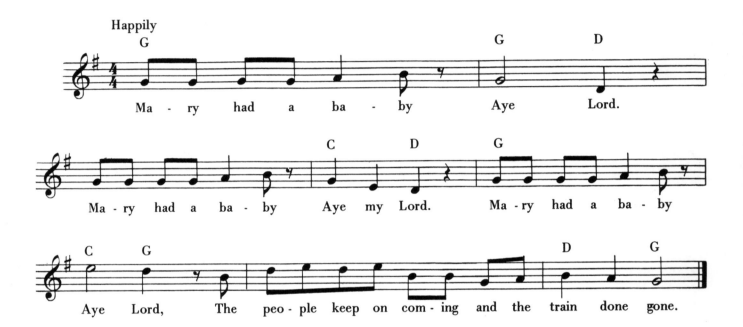

Mary had a baby, aye Lord,
Mary had a baby, aye my Lord,
Mary had a baby, aye Lord,
The people keep a-coming and the train done gone.

What name did she name him? Aye Lord, etc.

Named him Jesus, aye Lord, etc.

Where was he born? Aye Lord, etc.

He was born in Bethlehem, aye Lord, etc.

Where did she lay him? Aye Lord, etc.

She laid him in a manger, aye Lord, etc.

(Any number of verses can be added.)

Bye Bye Baby

This song was collected by Cecil Sharp from a Mrs. Sarah Ann Elizabeth Thomas at Dooley, Virginia.

Cecil Sharp, known for his collection of English folk songs, visited the southern Appalachian mountain region of North America in 1916, 1917, and 1918 and collected well over a thousand songs and ballads.

One of the interesting things about this collection is that he found the same traditional airs that he had found in England, but they were more lively and more frequently sung; and the inhabitants, tucked away from the rest of North America, spoke a language which was more English than American. *Appalachian*

Sustained and gently moving

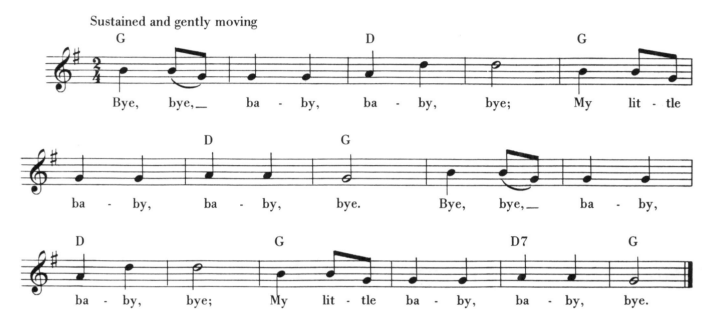

Bye, bye,— ba - by, ba - by, bye; My lit - tle ba - by, ba - by, bye. Bye, bye,— ba - by, ba - by, bye; My lit - tle ba - by, ba - by, bye.

Bye, bye, baby, baby, bye;
My little baby, baby, bye.
Bye, bye, baby, baby, bye;
My little baby, baby, bye.

The Mocking Bird

This version of the lullaby was recorded by Moe Asch. The words up to verse five are included, with very slight variations, in various collections of English nursery rhymes. Two versions were collected by Cecil Sharp, one in Virginia and one in North Carolina. Still another version has been collected recently by Kenneth Peacock, and can be found in his *Songs of Newfoundland Outports Vol. 1.* In the Peacock version a "rocking horse" and a "brand new frock" follow the reference to the diamond ring, which makes this version much closer to the English original. *Appalachian*

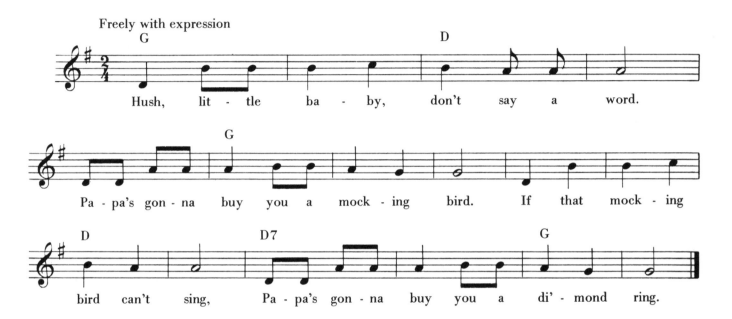

Hush, lit - tle ba - by, don't say a word. Pa - pa's gon - na buy you a mock - ing bird. If that mock - ing bird can't sing, Pa - pa's gon - na buy you a di' - mond ring.

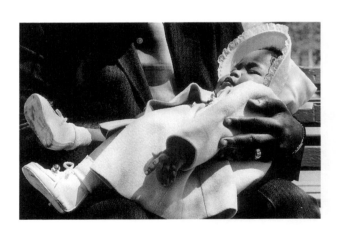

Hush little baby, don't say a word;
Papa's gonna buy you a mocking bird.

If that mocking bird can't sing,
Papa's gonna buy you a diamond ring.

If that di'mond ring turns to brass,
Papa's gonna buy you a looking glass.

If that looking glass gets broke,
Papa's gonna buy you a billy-goat.

If that billy-goat don't pull,
Papa's gonna buy you a cart and bull.

If that cart and bull turn over,
Papa's gonna buy you a dog named Rover.

If that dog named Rover won't bark,
Papa's gonna buy you a horse and cart.

If that horse and cart fall down,
You'll be the sweetest little one in town.

British Isles

The Wee Little Croodin Doo

"Lord Rendal," one of the best known and most widely sung of the folk ballads, is reflected in this imagined conversation between the baby and its mother. Although it has been included because the authors could not resist its charm and humor, it could not really be classified as a lullaby! *Scottish*

Where hae ye been the livelong day,
My wee little croodin doo?
I've been to see my stepmother,
Mammy, mak' my bed noo.

And what did your stepmother give you to eat,
My wee little croodin doo?
She gave me a wee wee blue fish,
Mammy, mak' my bed noo.

And what did ye do to the bones of the fish,
My wee little croodin doo?
I gave them to my wee wee dog,
Mammy, mak' my bed noo.

And what did your dog when he'd eat of the bones,
My wee little croodin doo?
He stretched his wee leggies and died
Mammy, as I do noo!

Dance A Baby Diddy

Although this song is included in the nursery rhyme lullabies it is really a dandling song, a song sung while baby is fed and played with before he is put in the cradle. There are many dandling songs which are often sung instead of lullabies.

This particular rhyme was included in the performance of an old Italian wayfaring puppet showman by the name of Piccini who gave Punch and Judy shows in England about 1780. *English*

With joy

Dance a ba - by did - dy,__ What can Mam -my do wid - e?__

Sit in her lap, Give it some pap, And dance a ba - by did - dy.__

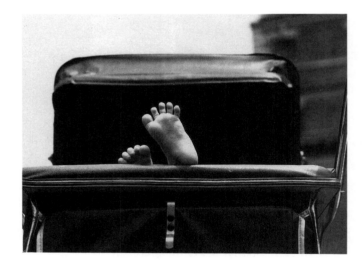

Dance a baby diddy,
What can Mammy do wid'e?
Sit in her lap, give it some pap,
And dance a baby diddy.

Dance To Your Daddy

This lullaby, or dandling song, is one of the many folk songs collected by Cecil Sharp from the County of Berkshire in England, although the reference to fish suggests a sea-coast origin. The song has a playful jigging rhythm and promises rewards to the baby, when his father returns home. By the time the second verse is sung the baby must be nearly asleep or very contented, for mother is dreaming of his future and no longer needs to hold his attention.

Other versions of this song are well known in Scotland and Northern England and it is found in the *Newcastle Song Book of Fordyce*, which was published about 1842.   *English*

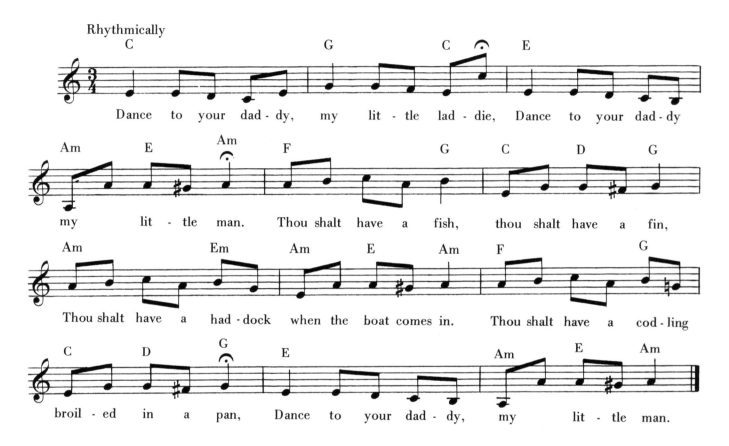

Dance to your Daddy, my little laddie,
Dance to your Daddy, my little man.
Thou shalt have a fish, thou shalt have a fin,
Thou shalt have a haddock when the boat comes in.
Thou shalt have a codling broiléd in a pan,
Dance to your Daddy, my little man.

Dance to your Daddy, my little laddie,
Dance to your Daddy, my little lamb.
When thou art a man and fit to take a wife,
Thou shalt choose a maid and love her all your life.
She shall be your lassie, thou shalt be her man,
Dance to your Daddy, my little lamb.

Newcastle Lullaby

This is probably a dandling song rather than a lullaby, learned by Mrs. Harrison of Newcastle from her old Scotch nurse.

Newcastle upon Tyne is in northeast England in the county of Northumberland which borders on Scotland. This lullaby was collected by A. G. Gilchrist.   *English*

With a strong sense of rhythm

Sleep bon - nie bairn - ie be - hind the cas - tle, By! By!

By! By! Thou shalt have a gold - en ap - ple, By! By! By! By!

This is better with no accompaniment

Sleep bonnie bairnie behind the castle,
By! By! By! By!
Thou shalt have a golden apple,
By! By! By! By!

Suo-Gân

LULLABY

The best known Welsh traditional songs are the flowing, complex melodies, such as *David of the White Rock*, which originated from the professional bards and harpists. This lullaby is a folksong with a simple melody and a more restricted melodic compass, whose written version dates from the eighteenth century. *Welsh*

Hun - a blen - tyn, ar fy myn- wes, Clyd a chyn - nes yd - ya hon;
Sleep my ba - by on my bo - som, Close - ly nest - le safe and warm;

Breich - iau mam syn dyn am dan - at, Car - iad mam sy dan fy mron,
Moth - er wake-ful watch - es o'er you, Round you fold - ed moth - er's arm

Ni chaiff dim am - har uth gyn - tun, Ni wna un - dyn â thi gam;
Sweet, there's noth -ing near can hurt you, Noth - ing threat - ens here your rest;

Hun - a'n daw - el an - nayl blen tyn Hun - a'n twyn ar fron dy fam.
Sleep my ba - by, Sleep and fear not, Sleep you sweet - ly on my breast.

Huna blentyn, ar fy mynwes,
Clyd a chynnes ydyw hon;
Breichiau mam syn dyn am danat,
Cariad mam sy dan fy mron,
Ni chaiff dim amharu'th gyntun,
Ni wna undyn â thi gam;
Huna'n dawel annwyl blentyn,
Huna'n fwyn ar fron dy fam.

Hun'an dawel heno huna,
Hun'an fwyn, y tlws ei lun;
Pam yr wyt yn awr yn gwenu,
Gwanu'n dirion yn dy hun?
Ai angylion fry sŷn gwenu

*Sleep my baby on my bosom,
Closely nestle safe and warm;
Mother wakeful, watches o'er you,
Round you folded mother's arm.
Sweet there's nothing near can hurt you,
Nothing threatens here your rest;
Sleep my baby, sleep and fear not,
Sleep you sweetly on my breast.*

*Lulla lulla sweetly slumber,
Mother's treasure, slumber deep;
Lulla, lulla, now you're smiling,
Smiling, dear one, through your sleep.
Say are angels bending o'er you*

Arnat ti yn gwenu'n llon.
Tithau'n gwenu'n ôl dan huno,
Huno'n dawel ar fy mron?

Paid ag ofni, dim ond deilen,
Gura, gura ar y ddôr;
Paid ag ofni ton fach unig.
Sua, sua ar lan y môr;
Huna blentyn, nid ces yma
Ddim i roddi iti fraw;
Gwena'n dawel yn fy mynwes
Ar yr engyl gwynion draw.

Smiling down from heaven above?
Is that heavenly smile your answer?
Love from dreamland answering love?

Hush my treasure, 'tis a leaflet
Beating, beating, on the door;
Hush my pretty, 'tis a ripple,
Lapping, lapping, on the shore.
Mother watches, nought can harm you,
Angel warders gather nigh;
Blessed angels, bending o'er you,
Sing your lulla, lullaby.

Croon

Like all croons, the phrases follow the natural rise and fall of the breath, and suggest sighing or half speaking rather than singing. This was collected by A. G. Gilchrist, from his grandfather. *Scottish*

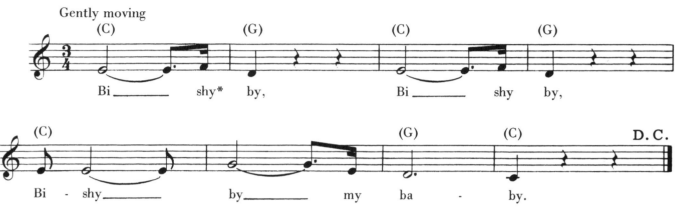

Bi_____ shy* by, Bi_____ shy by,
Bi - shy_____ by_____ my ba - by.

* S has z sound, as in Irish "Husheen".
This is better with no accompaniment.

Bi-shy by, by-shy bi,
Bi-shy by, my baby.

Can Ye Sew Cushions

This well known lullaby appeared as a nursery song in the Scots' Musical Museum in 1797, and was submitted by Robert Burns nearly a century later. The change in the mother's mood as she sings is shown very clearly by the change of rhythm. The song opens with long soothing phrases as the mother thinks of her "wee lamb," and then as she becomes worried about how she can feed all her other "wee lambs," the rhythm quickens and becomes worried and impatient. *Scottish*

O can ye sew cushions, and can ye sew sheets?
And can ye sing ba-lu-lo when the bairn greets?
And hie and baw birdie, and hie and baw lamb,
And hie and baw birdie my bonnie wee lamb.

Refrain
Hee-o-wee-o what will I do wi' ye?
Blacks the life that I lead wi' you.
Many o' you, little for to gi'e you,
Hee-o-wee-o what will I do wi' you?

I've placed my cradle, on yon holly top,
And aye as the wind blows my cradle will rock.
O hush-a-ba baby, o ba-lily-loo,
And hee and ba birdie my bonnie wee doo.

Repeat refrain.

Ksihmul Cradle Croon

The Hebrides, tiny islands off the northwest coast of Scotland, are famous for their physical beauty, but also for their incredibly lovely folk songs.

They have been collected by the Kennedy Fraser family, Marjorie Kennedy Fraser, Kenneth Macleod, and Patuffa Kennedy Fraser, all musicians and all with a poet's love of the islands and an understanding of the particular phase of civilization which they represented.

The Hebridean croons or mouth-music songs were considered more important than a lullaby, for they not only helped the baby to go to sleep, but exerted a kind of magic which strengthened the little one to whom the song was sung. It is no mere accident that in the Scots-Gaelic the word for lullaby "taladh" also means "enchantment." This kind of croon was originally made up to sing to a particular baby who belonged to a family of some importance. There were, however, other equally beautiful but less elaborate croons which were sung by everyone.

This particular croon was collected from Annie Johnson of the Glen, Barra, and arranged for harp and voice by Patuffa Kennedy Fraser. It was attributed to Nic Iaon Acidh, the woman who made the song "Kishmul's Galley." It was said to have been sung by her to the baby Ruari Macneill, heir to Kishmul. *Hebridean*

(repeat words of verse one)

Hee-o-ho-ro, mo Ruarachan,
Ho ree-o-ho-ro, mo Ruarachan,
Hee-o-ho-ro, mo Ruarachan,
Mo Nial-lach-an beag, mo chubh-rach-an.*

Hee-o-ho ree, hu-o-ho-ro,
Mo Nial-lach-an beag, mo chubh-rach-an,
Hee-o-ho, ree-o-ho, ru-o-ho-ro,
Mo Nial-lach-an beag, mo chubh-rach-an.

Hee-o-ho-ro, mo Ru-ar-ach-an,
Mo Nial-lach-an beag, mo chubh-rach-an.

(repeat from beginning)

*
Ru pronounce Roo, *Nial-lach* pronounce Nee-al,
Beag pronounce Peck, *Chubh* pronounce Hoo.

Hò Hò Bho Laidi Bheag

A simple lullaby collected by Polly Hitchcock much more recently than those collected by the Kennedy Frasers.   *Hebridean*

REFRAIN:

Hò ho bho laidi bheag,
Hò ho bho éileadh,
Hò ho bho laidi bheag,
Hò ho bho éileadh.

Hò ho bho laidi bheag
Hò ho bho éileadh,
Ged nach'eil thu ach òg bidh
Gu ed iran déidhort

REFRAIN:

Hò ho bho laidi bheag
Hò ho bho laidi,
Hò ho bho laidi bheag,
Hò ho bho éileadh.

Hò ho bho laidi bheag,
Hò ho bho éileadh,
Although you are very young,
Many will like you.

'S'a bhean a gheibh Domhnuill
Bidh ciòr aie'airté'eile,
Bidh iasgair Bidh sealgair;
Bidh marbhaich' an fhéidh.

Refrain

And the wife Donald marries
Will be most important,
For he'll be a Fisherman
And a Deer Hunter.

Refrain

Codail A Leanb

THE GARTAN MOTHER'S LULLABY

This lullaby with its tender and beautiful melody comes from County Donegal. Herbert Hughes reminds us in his preface to *Irish Country Songs* that over a thousand years ago Ireland was the most highly educated country in Western Europe and as a consequence its contemporary literature and folk music still have their own peculiar qualities. Folk melodies like this one combine rare beauty and distinction with more variety of mood than can be found in any other folk music. *Irish*

Codail a leanb, tá'n beacog búide
Ag crónan an clap soluis ciuin.
Seo cugáinn aoibeall na carraige léité
Cun an tsaogaill do cur cun suain.
A leanbain O mo rún mo sóg,
Mo grád 'gus dúll mo croide.
Do suantraige mall ag na gcreagair á gabail
' Gus an teine ag dul ineág.

Dóirce anois is sceac'n fir glais
As radarc le caipíní ceoige.
' Seoläid a báidín béid siabra go maidín,
Ar an bportac reáltac beoda
A leanbáin O tá an gealac bán,
Lán fá máoie le drúct,
' Gus golann go bog an suan-port do clos,
A gabaim mo graídin duit.

Sleep, O babe, for the red bee hums,
The silent twilight falls,
Eeval from the grey rock comes,
To wrap the world in thrall!
A lyan van o, my child my joy,
My love and heart's desire,
The crickets sing you lullaby
Beside the dying fire.

Dusk is drawn, and the green man's thorn
Is wreathed in rings of fog.
Sheevra sails his boat till morn
Upon the starry bog,
A lyan van o, the paly moon
Hath brimm'd her cusp in dew,
And weeps to hear the sad sleep tune
I sing O love to you.

Ushag Veg Ruy

LITTLE RED BIRD

The published collection of many folk songs is small. This lullaby, arranged by Arnold Foster with an English translation by Mona Douglas, has been taken from A. W. Moore's *Many Ballads and Music.*

The melody is of exceptional beauty. In it one can feel the swaying of the tree branches and the rise and fall of the wind on the moor as the mother rocks her baby to the story of the little red bird. *Manx*

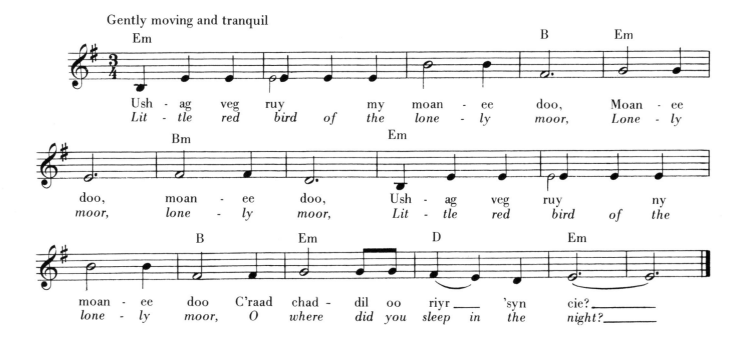

REFRAIN

Ushag veg ruy ny moanee doo,
Moanee doo, moanee doo,
Ushag veg ruy ny moanee doo,
C'raad chaddil oo riyr 'syn cie?

Nagh chaddil mish riyr er baare y crouw,
Baare y crouw, baare y crouw,
Lesh fliag hey tuittym er dagh cheu,
As ogh! my chadley cha treih.

Refrain—Ushag veg ruy, etc.

Nagh chaddil mish riyr er baare yn dress,
Baare yn dress, baare yn dress,
Tra va'n gheay sheidey veh gymmyrkey lhee
As ogh! my chadley cha treih.

Refrain—Ushag veg ruy, etc.

Nagh chaddil mish riyr er baare y tonn,
Baare y tonn, baare y tonn,
Myr shimey mac dooinney cadley roym,
As ogh! my chadley cha treih.

REFRAIN

Little red bird of the lonely moor,
Lonely moor, lonely moor,
Little red bird of the lonely moor,
O where did you sleep in the night?

Out on a gorse bush dark and wide,
Dark and wide, dark and wide,
Swift rain was falling on every side,
O hard was my sleep last night.

Refrain

Did I not sleep on the swaying briar,
Swaying briar, swaying briar,
Tossing about as the wind rose higher,
O little I slept last night!

Refrain

Did I not sleep on the cold wave's crest,
Cold wave's crest, cold wave's crest,
Where many a man has taken his rest,
And O! my sleep was too light.

Refrain

O chaddil mish riyr eddyr daa ghuillag,
Eddyr daa ghuillag, eddyr daa ghuillag,
Myr cadley yn oikan er kneeag y vumming,
As ogh! my chadley cha treih.

Refrain

Wrapped in two leaves I lay at ease,
Lay at ease, lay at ease,
As sleeps the young babe on its mother's knees,
O sweet was my sleep last night!

I've Found My Bonny Babe A Nest

This lullaby taken from the *Petrie Collection* can be found in *Songs of Erin*, edited by Sir Charles Villiers Stanford, with words by Charles Percival Graves. It probably belongs to a very early period of Irish music and it has the artlessly beautiful melody which characterizes most of the Irish lullabies.

George Petrie was the first really important Celtic folk song collector. He collected over two thousand tunes from all over Ireland and was accompanied by his friend, Eugene O'Curry, who transcribed the words and later translated them into English. *Irish*

I've found my bonny babe a nest,
On slumber tree.
I'll rock you here to rosy rest,
Astore Machree.
Oh lulla lo sing all the leaves,
On slumber tree,
Till everything that hurts or grieves,
Afar must flee.

Hush-A-Bye Baby, On The Tree Top

This is probably the best known lullaby in England and North America. The date of both words and melody are uncertain, although the words were first found in printed form in *Mother Goose's Melodies*, dated 1765. The melody, a variant of Lillibulero, better known now as the nursery song "There Was an Old Woman Tossed Up in a Basket," is said to be an adaptation of one of Henry Purcell's melodies. If this is correct the melody must have been written between 1658 and 1695.

The alternative melody which is now sung in North America to the words, and has continued to gain in popularity, is attributed to a Mrs. Effie Canning Carlton of America, who composed it in 1874. It first appeared in printed form in Denman Thompson's *The Old Homestead*, with the word "rockaby" substituted for the older "hushaby."   *English*

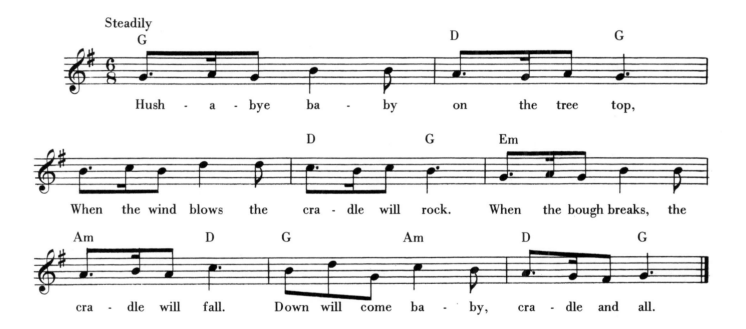

Hush-a-bye baby on the tree top,
When the wind blows the cradle will rock.
When the bough breaks, the cradle will fall,
Down will come baby, cradle and all.

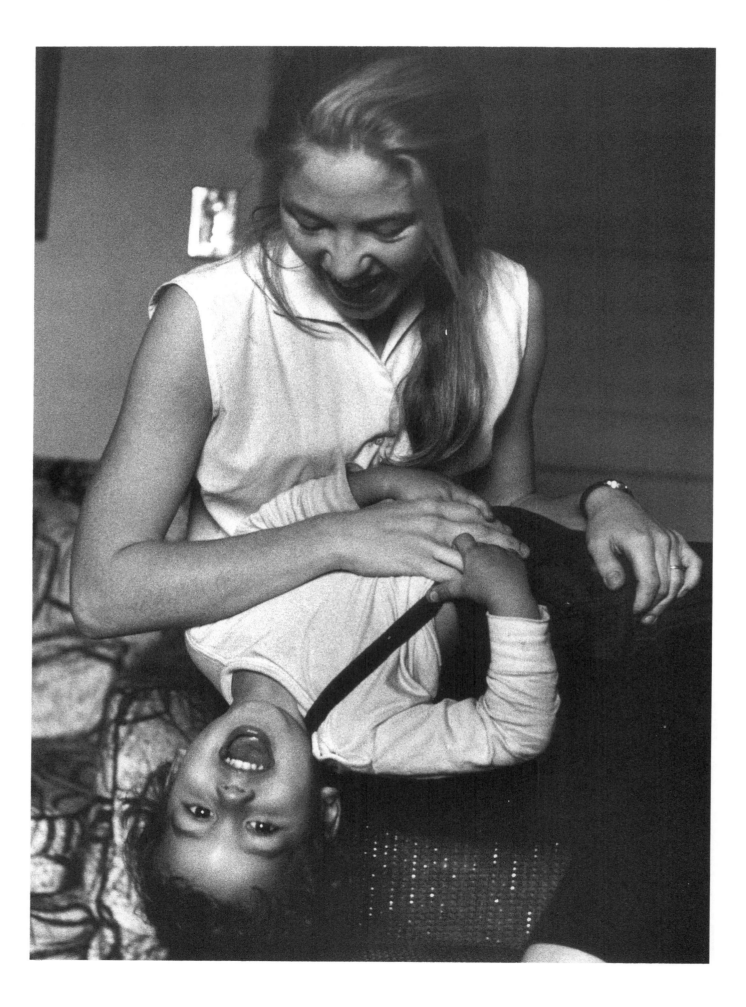

Scandinavia & Northwestern Europe

Naa Ska'en Liten Faa Sova Soa Södt

THE CRADLE IS READY, AND THERE YOU SHALL SLEEP

A lullaby with a melody that curves and sways like the branches of a tree moving gently in the wind. Here there is no fear that the "branch will break." *Norwegian*

Naa ska' en li - ten faa so - va soa södt,
The cra - dle is rea - dy and there you shall sleep,

Vög - ga staar re - je te baa - ne,
Safe and so warm lit - tle ba - by.

Der ska' en lig - ge saa vart aa saa blödt,
An - gels shall come and stand close - ly to keep,

Trygt - kan de so - va de baa - ne,
Watch o - ver you lit - tle ba - by.

Ro Ro so - va saa södt, Guds en - gel tar va - re paa baa - ne.
(Bye Bye) now go to sleep, So sweet - ly to sleep lit - tle ba - by.

Naa ska'en liten faa sova saa södt,
Vögga staar reje te baane,
Der ska'en ligge saa vart aa saa blödt
Trygt kan de sova de baane,
Ro Ro sova saa södt,
Guds engel tar vare paa baane.
Ro ro sova saa södt,
Guds engel tar vare paa baane.

(repeat)

The cradle is ready and there you shall sleep,
Safe and so warm little baby.
Angels shall come and stand closely to keep,
Watch over you little baby.
Bye bye now go to sleep,
So sweetly to sleep little baby.
Bye bye now go to sleep,
So sweetly to sleep little baby.

(repeat)

46

Ro Ro Relte

HUSH BABY HUSH

Here baby is promised a variety of colourful clothes, with
no conditions attached!   *Norwegian*

Ro,   ro,   rel   -   te,   Kjø - pe,   baa - ne   bel - te,
Hush,   hush,   ba - by,   Moth - er's   going   to   buy   you

Nytt   bel - te,   ny - e   sko,   Ron - da   fleng - jé
New   belt,   and   pair   of   shoes,   Ti - ny   cap   and

trøy - a   go,   Aa   ei   li - tor   hu - ve.
dress   of   blue,   And   a   lit - tle   jack - et.

Ro, ro, relte,
Kjøpe baane belte,
Nytt belte, nye sko,
Ronda flengjé trøya go,
Aa ei litor huve.

Hush hush, baby,
Mother's going to buy you
New belt and pair of shoes,
Tiny cap and dress of blue,
And a little jacket.

Hist Hyor Vejen Slär En Bugt

MOTHER AND CHILD

This lullaby, known as "Mother and Child," has words
by Hans Christian Andersen and is set to an old Danish folk
tune. *Danish*

Keep moving but very peaceful

Hist, hyor ve - jen slär en bugt,____ Lig - ger der et hus så smukt.
See____ where the road____ bends, a Tin - y house stands at the end.

Vaeg - gene lidt____ skae - ve stå rud - erne er____ gan - ske små,
Crook - ed walls and win - dows small Doors that hard - ly close at all.

Dör - en syn - ker halvt - i knae, Hun - den göe - r, det lille krae,
Dog he barks, bad lit - tle thing, In the eaves the swal - lows sing.

Un - der ta - get sval - er kvidre, sol - en syn - ker - og så vid're.
And the sun - shine will not last, For the sun is set - ting____ fast.

Hist, hvor vejen slår en bugt,
Ligger der et hus så smukt.
Vaeggene lidt skaeve stå,
Ruderne er ganske små,
Dören synker halvt i knae,
Hunden göer, det lille krae,
Under taget svaler kvidre,
Solen synker-og så vid're.

I den röde aftensol
Sidder moder i sin stol;
Kinden luer dobbelt röd,
Harnet har hun på sit skod.
Drengen er så frisk og sund,
Aebekinden röd og rund!
Se, hvor hun i spög ham banker
På de söde pusselanker.

Katten står og krummer ryg,
Men forstyrres af en myg;
Barsk han den med poten slåi
Og igen som hofmand star.
Moder klapper barnets kind;
Se, hvor södt det sover ind,
Drömmer om de engle smukke
I sin lille, paene vugge.

See where the road bends,
A tiny house stands at the end.
Crooked walls and windows small,
Doors that hardly close at all.
Dog he barks, bad little thing,
In the eaves the swallows sing.
And the sunshine will not last,
For the sun is setting fast.

In the rosy evening sun
Mother sits, the charming one.
Apple red her cheeks must be,
And her son is on her knee.
He is strong as if he grew
Like red rosy apples too.
Spanks his hands in joyful game
'Til he cries "again, again."

There stands cat with arched back
Troubled by a stinging gnat,
Boldly hits it with his paw,
Then stands stately as before.
Mother pats her baby's cheek,
See how soon he falls asleep?
Dreams of angels in the skies
As within his crib he lies.

Vyssa Lulla Litet Barn

HUSHABYE MY LITTLE BABE

An engaging lullaby that offers the typical reward of
something sweet to eat if baby goes to sleep! *Swedish*

Gently moving

Vys - sa lul - la, li - tet barn, För en li - ten
Hush - a - bye, my lit - tle babe. For a lit - tle

ka - ka; Kan ag ing - en ka - ka lå
su - gar cake. If a cake I can - not find,

Skall jag lå - ta vag - gan stå, Lå - ta bar - ne grå - ta.
Then the cra - dle I'll not mind, Leave the babe a - cry - ing.

Vyssa lulla, litet barn,
För en liten kaka;
Vyssa lulla, litet barn,
For en liten kaka;
Kan'ag ingen kaka lå
Skall jag låta vaggan stå,
Låta barne gråta.

Hush-a-bye, my little babe,
For a little sugar cake.
Hush-a-bye, my little babe,
For a little sugar cake.

If a cake I cannot find,
Then the cradle I'll not mind,
Leave the babe a-crying.

50

Mana Gallaka Noukat

This lullaby, sung by Inga M. Haetta, simply says that children ought to sleep. It is a Joik song, which is now the only type of song that Lapps sing. Joiking is typical of the mountain people. It is like yodelling, and is sung in a sitting position with the head bent, as though sitting beside a herd on the mountains. There are no words and the singing technique is to fill the lungs with air, sing until it is exhausted, take another breath and continue in this way until the song is ended.

Every melody describes some living person or animal and in addition each person has his own melody. This is like a portrait of the person who makes it up, and it is his own and does not change. There are masculine and feminine melodies and practically all of them are pentatonic. Many songs have a magical background and some were used during Shamanistic rites, as before conversion to Christianity the religion of the Lapps like that of the Northern Asiatic tribes was Shamanism.
Lapp

Man - a gall - a - ka nou - kat, Lu - li, lu - li, lu - li loo.

Lu - li lu - li lu - li - loo, Lu - li lu - li lu - li lu - loo.

Mana gallaka noukat,
Lu-li, lu-li, lu-li loo.
Lu-li, lu-li, lu-li loo,
Lu-li, lu-li, lu-lilu loo.

Sofdu Únga Ástin Mín

SLEEP MY DARLING BABY SLEEP

Two versions of this lullaby are given, and version "B" is particularly lovely. Its modal character suggests that it is the earlier of the two versions. Icelandic folk music was transcribed at a very early date so that practically all folk melodies which are sung can be found in a printed form. As a result Icelandic people are well acquainted with their folk music. *Icelandic*

VERSION A

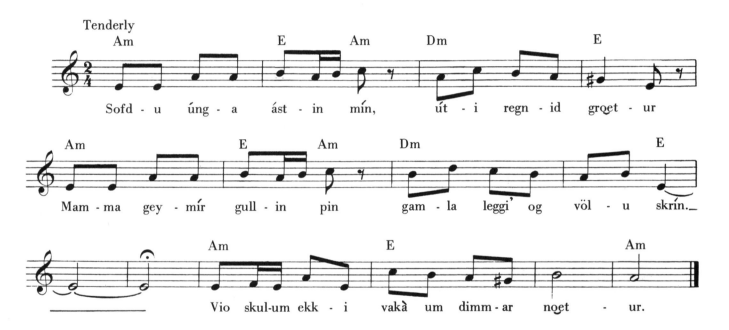

Sofdu únga ástin mín, úti regnio groetur
Mama geymír gullin pin, gamla leggi'og völu skrín.
Vio skulum ekki vakà um dimmar noetur.

Sing this verse to both melodies:

Sleep my darling baby sleep, rain is gently falling.
Mother will thy treasure keep, hidden where the
*   shadows creep.*
Hush thee my baby, night for rest is calling.

52

VERSION B

Sofd - u úng - a ást - in mín, út - i regn - id
Sleep my dar - ling ba - by sleep, rain is gen - tle

groet - ur Mam - ma geym - ir gull - in pin gam - la leggi og
fall - ing Mo - ther will thy treas - ures keep, hid - den where the

völ - u skrín. Vio skul - um ekk - i vakà um dimm - ar noet - ur.
shad - ows creep, so húsh thee my ba - by, night for rest is call - ing.

Sofdu únga ástin mín, úti regnið groetur
Mama geymir gullin pin, gamla leggi'og volu skrín.
Vio skulum ekki vakà um dimmar noetur.

Kehto Laula

CRADLE SONG

This cradle song was recalled by a young man, Adolf Stark, and his wife, Karelia, who emigrated to America from their home town of Enso, Finland. As a boy Adolf Stark used to play the violin and the Finnish harp, known as the Kantele, and both he and his wife have taken an interest in the folk songs of their country. *Finnish*

Pium paum, kehto heilahtaä,
Ja lapsi via toinna nukahtaä
Pium paum Äiti laulaa vain
Kun sydan kápyánsá tundittaä.

Pium paum Viulu vingahtaä
Ja nuoret karkeloihin kiiruhtaä
Pium paum nauti elämaä
Sillain kun se sulle hymyaä.

Pium paum kerran kajahtaä
Tuo kirkon kello sulle ilmoittaä
Pois pois henki vaeltaä
Ja ruumis mullan alla majan saä.

Pium paum, cradle swaying on,
How innocently baby falls asleep.
Pium paum, cradle swinging on,
While the mother sings her cradle song.

Pium paum, sound of fiddle creaks,
In haste the happy youngsters dancing go.
Pium paum, go enjoy your life,
While you're young and it still smiles at you.

Pium paum, some day bells will clang,
The church's bell will one day end your toil,
Then will your soul roam on,
While your body rests beneath the soil.

Western & Southern Europe

Schlaf, Kindlein Schlaf — *German*
Schlaf In Guter Ruh — *German*
Do Do Kindje Van De Minne — *Dutch*
Hoe Laat Is't? — *Dutch*
Fais Dodo — *French*
Fais Dodo Lola La Belle — *Breton*
A La Nanita Nana — *Spanish*
Dodo, L'enfant Dors — *Belgian*
Nânez Binamêye Poyète — *Walloon*
Fi La Nanae, Mi Bel Fiole — *Italian*
Ró Ró — *Portuguese*
Κοιμᾶται τὸ μωροῦτσκό μου — *Greek*
Ela Ypne — *Greek*
Nam, Nam — *Maltese*

Schlaf, Kindlein Schlaf

SLEEP BABY SLEEP

This is probably one of the world's best known lullabies and there are many different versions of this lovely little melody. There is an arrangement by Johannes Brahms for Schumann's children that can be found in his book of folk songs for children. One version of this lullaby was incorporated by Wagner into his *Siegfried-Idyl.* *German*

VERSION A

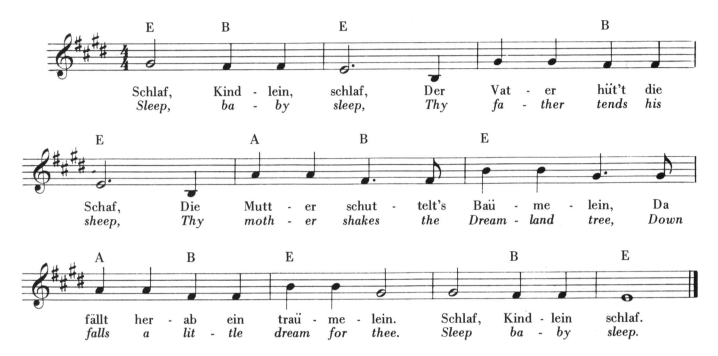

Schlaf, Kind - lein, schlaf, Der Vat - er hüt't die
Sleep, ba - by sleep, Thy fa - ther tends his

Schaf, Die Mutt - er schut - telt's Baü - me - lein, Da
sheep, Thy moth - er shakes the Dream - land tree, Down

fällt her - ab ein traü - me - lein. Schlaf, Kind - lein schlaf.
falls a lit - tle dream for thee. Sleep ba - by sleep.

Schlaf, kindlein, schlaf.
Der Vater hüt't die schaf,
Die Mutter schuttelt's Baümelein,
Da fällt herab ein traümelein.
Schlaf, kindlein, schlaf.

Schlaf, kindlein, schlaf.
Am Himmel ziehn die schaf
Die Sternlein sind die Lämmerlein,
Der Mond, der ist das Shäferlein,
Schlaf, kindlein, schlaf.

Schlaf, kindlein, schlaf.
Geh' fort und hüt die schaf
Geh' fort du schwarzes hündelein,
Und weck' mir nicht men kind'lein
Schlaf, kindlein, schlaf.

Sleep, baby sleep,
Thy father tends his sheep,
Thy mother shakes the dreamland tree,
Down falls a little dream for thee.
Sleep, baby sleep.

Sleep, baby sleep,
The large stars are the sheep,
The little stars are lambs I guess,
The golden moon the shepherdess.
Sleep, baby sleep.

Sleep, baby sleep,
Away and tend thy sheep,
Away thou black dog fierce and wild,
And do not harm my little child.
Sleep, baby sleep.

Schlaf, Kind - lein, schlaf. Der Vat - er hüt't die
Sleep, *ba - by* *sleep,* *Thy* *fa - ther* *tends* *his*

schlaf, Die Mut - ter schut - telt's Baü - me - lein, Da
sheep, *Thy* *moth - er* *shakes* *the* *Dream - land* *tree,* *Down*

fällt her - ab ein traü - me - lein. Schlaf, Kind - lein schlaf.
falls *a* *lit - tle* *dream* *for thee.* *Sleep,* *ba - by* *sleep.*

Schlaf, In Guter Ruh

SLEEP IN GOOD PEACE

This lullaby requires a mother with some real vocal ability!
As a lullaby it is a little worrying, for mother keeps reminding
baby of all kinds of unpleasant things, before saying sweetly,
"but never mind, you go to sleep." Everything comes right by
the time the last verse is reached but perhaps by this time baby
is asleep! *German*

At a moderate pace

1. Schlaf in gut - er Ruh,_____ Tu die Aeu - ge - lein
   Sleep in good peace,_____ Close your wake - ful

zu,_____ Hoe - re wie - der Re - gen faellt, Hoe - re wie
eyes,_____ Lis - ten to__ the fall - ing rain, Hear the next

nach - bars Huend - chen bellt. Huend - chen hat den Mann ge
door__ dog bark a - gain. He has bitten a beg - gar

biss - en, Hat des Bet - tlers Kleid zer - ris - sen, Bet - tler
man, He has torn the beg - gar's cloth - ing, Beg - gar

laeuft der Pfor - te zu. Schlaf in sues - ser Ruh._____
man has got a - way. Sleep in sweet - est peace._____

Schlaf in guter ruh,
Tu die aeugelein zu,
Hoere wieder regen faellt,
Hoere wie nachbars huendchen bellt.
Huendchen hat den mann gebissen,
Hat des bettlers kleid zerrissen,
Bettler laeuft der pforte zu
Schlaf in suesser ruh.

Still mein suesses kind,
Draussen weht der wind.
Haeschen, haeschen spitzt das ohr,
Sieht aus langem gras hervor,
Jaeger kommt im gruenen kléide
Jagt das haeschen aus der weide,
Haeschen laeuft geschwind, geschwind.
Still, mein suesses kind.

Kannst nun ruhig sein,
Bettler kehrt schon ein,
Haeschen schlaeft auf stacheldorn,
Haeschen liegt nun schon im korn,
Taeubchen fuettert seine jungen,
Voeglein hat nun ausgesungen,
Mued' ist alles gross und klein,
Schlaf nun ruhig ein.

Sleep in good peace,
Close your wakeful eyes,
Listen to the falling rain,
Hear the next door dog bark again.
He has bitten a beggar man,
He has torn the beggar's clothing,
Beggar man has got away.
Sleep in sweetest peace.

My sweet child,
Still the wind blows outside,
Baby rabbit shows his ears,
Peering through the grass, he fears
The hunter dressed in green, who chases
Baby rabbit from the meadow,
But he runs so fast, so fast,
Still he runs sweet child.

Now you can be peaceful,
For the beggar man comes back,
And the rabbit sleeps safe again
For he rests in fields of grain.
Doves will feed their tiny fledglings,
And the birds will end their singing,
Everyone is sleepy now,
Fall asleep in peace.

Do Do Kindje Van De Minne

DO DO MOTHER'S LITTLE LOVED ONE

This lullaby was written down in Mechelen about 1900. The melody was constructed from a four-bar fragment learnt in Ghent by the collector Van Duyse. Indications that it is very old and Flemish rather than Dutch, are provided by the words *minne* and *vaak*. *Minne*, although translated here as mother, really means wet nurse or Nanny and a wet nurse would only have been employed in the more elaborate households of Flanders. *Vaak* is old Flemish and means drowsy or still, in the sense of nodding off. *Klaas-Vaak* is the equivalent of sandman. *Dutch*

Do, do kindje van de minne,
Slaap en doe je oogjes toe.
Heb je gene vaak, je moet niet slapen,
Heb je gene honger, je moet niet gapen.
Do, do kindje van de minne,
Slaap en doe je oogjes toe.

Do, do, mother's little loved one,
Close your misty eyes and sleep.
If you are not still, you won't be sleeping,
If you are not hungry, don't be weeping.
Do, do, mother's little loved one,
Close your misty eyes in sleep.

Hoe Laat Is't?

WHAT TIME IS IT?

This lullaby belongs in comfortable circumstances and moves to the solemn ticking of the grandfather's clock. There is clearly nothing to worry about, and one pictures a rosy-cheeked baby nodding in the happy security of a Dutch home.
Dutch

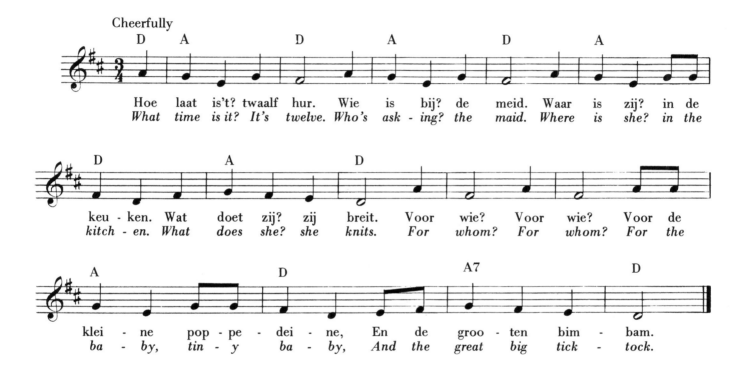

Hoe laat is't? twaalf hur. Wie is bij? de meid. Waar is zij? in de
What time is it? It's twelve. Who's ask - ing? the maid. Where is she? in the

keu - ken. Wat doet zij? zij breit. Voor wie? Voor wie? Voor de
kitch - en. What does she? she knits. For whom? For whom? For the

klei - ne pop - pe - dei - ne, En de groo - ten bim - bam.
ba - by, tin - y ba - by, And the great big tick - tock.

Hoe laat is't? twaalf uur
Wie is bij? de meid.
Waar is zij? in de keuken.
Wat doet zij? zij breit.
Voor wie? voor wie?
Voor de kleine poppedeine
En den grooten bim bam.

What time is it? it's twelve.
Who's asking? the maid.
Where is she? in the kitchen.
What does she? she knits.
(literally, what is she doing?)
For whom? for whom?
For the baby, tiny baby,
And the great big tick tock.

Fais Dodo

GO TO SLEEP

This lullaby is well known and much loved, throughout France and French Canada. This version and the translation come from Alan Mills. *French*

Fais do-do, colas, mon p'tit frère,
Fais do-do, t'auras du lolo.

Maman est en haut, qui fait des gâteaux,
Papa est en bas qui fait du chocolait,

Fais do-do, colas, mon p'tit frère,
Fais do-do, t'auras du lolo.

Go to sleep, my sweet little brother,
Go to sleep, and you'll get a treat. *

Oh, Mother's upstairs, some cookies she'll bake,
And Father's downstairs, sweet chocolate to make.

Go to sleep, my sweet little brother,
Go to sleep, and you'll have a treat.

---

* 'Lolo' is a baby talk work for milk. It can also mean anything that baby especially likes

Fais Dodo Lola Ma Belle

GO TO SLEEP, LULLA MY DARLING

Brittany, because of its background of Celtic culture (which still lives in the Celtic language which they continue to speak), has a rather special contribution to make in the cultural field. This lullaby is well known in France, Belgium and Haiti, and in this version it is sung to French words. *Breton*

Fais do - do, lo - la ma bel - le, Fais do -
Go to sleep, lull - a my dar - ling, Go to

do,___ lo - la.___ Ton pè - re est lo - in, Ta
sleep___ lull - a.___ Thy fa - ther's a - wa - y, Thy

mè - re i - ci Qui ve - ille le son en -
moth - er is here To wa - tch his lit - tle

fant___ chér - i. Fait do - do, lo - la ma
chi - ld so dear. Go to sleep, lull - a my

bel - le, Fais do - do___ lo - la.___
dar - ling, Go to slee - p lull - a.___

Fais dodo, lola la belle,
Fais dodo, lola.
Ton père est loin,
Ta mère ici
Qui veille le son enfant chéri.
Fais dodo, lola la belle,
Fais dodo lola.

Fais dodo, lola la belle,
Fais dodo, lola.
Jadis elle a pleurée souvent,
Mais maintenant sourit gaiement.
Fais dodo, lola la belle,
Fais dodo, lola.

Go to sleep, lulla my darling,
Go to sleep lulla.
Thy father's away,
Thy mother is here
To watch his little child so dear.
Go to sleep, lulla my darling,
Go to sleep lulla.

Go to sleep, lulla my darling,
Go to sleep lulla.
Although she used to often weep,
She now smiles gaily (in her sleep).
Go to sleep, lulla my darling,
Go to sleep lulla.

A La Nanita Nana

ROCKABY BABY

In Spanish lullabies the name Jesus often occurs because this is a popular first name, and it therefore has no special religious significance. The modulation from the major to the minor key is also quite characteristic of many of their lullabies. This one with its curving melody and elaborate words is hauntingly tender. *Spanish*

Tenderly

A la na- ni- ta na- na, na- ni- ta
Rock- a- by ba- by, go to

e- a, na- ni- ta e- a, Mi Je- sús tie- ne
sleep now, go to sleep now, My lit- tle Je- sus

sue- ño, ben- di- to se- a, ben- di- to se- a. *Fine*
wants to go to sleep, God bless__ him,__ God__ bless him.

Fuen- te- ci- illa que cor- res cla- ra y so- no- ra,
Lit- tle flow- ing foun- tain, spark- ling and mu- si- cal,

Rui- se ñor- de la sel- va, can- tan- do llo- ras;
Night- in- gale of the woods __ cry-ing as you sing,

ca- llad mien- tras la cu- na se- ba- lan- ce- a
Hush while the cra- dle's sway- ing, sway- ing and swing- ing,

A la na- ni- ta na- na, na- ni- ta e- a.
Rock- a- by lit- tle ba- by, rock- a- by, go to sleep.

A la nanita nana, nanita ea nanita ea,
Mi Jesús tiene sueño bendito sea, bendito sea.

FIRST CHORUS:

Fuentecilla que corres clara y sonors,
Ruiseñor de la selva, cantando lloras;
Callad mientras la cuna se balancea,
A la nanita, nana, nanita ea

Manojito de rosasy de alelíes y de alelíes,
Qué es lo que estás soñando, qué te sonries, qué te
    sonries?

SECOND CHORUS:

Fuentecilla que corres, clara y sonora;
Ruiseñor de la selva, cantando lloras;
Cuáles son tus ensuenos? dilo, alma mia;
Cuáles son tus ensueños? dilo, alma mia.

Pajarillos y fuenites auras y brisas, auras y brisas;

Respetad ese sueño y esas sonrisas y esas sonrias

Rockaby baby, o go to sleep now, o go to sleep now,
My little Jesus wants to go to sleep, God bless him,
    God bless him.

FIRST CHORUS:

Little flowing fountain, sparkling and musical,
Nightingale of the woods crying as you sing,
Hush while the cradle's swaying, swaying and swinging,
Rockaby little baby, rockaby, go to sleep.

My little flower, like the roses, like the gilliflowers,
What are you dreaming of that makes you smile
    so sweetly?

SECOND CHORUS:

Little flowing fountain, sparkling and musical,
Nightingale of the woods crying as you sing,
What dream you of my baby, tell me my soul?
What dream you of my baby, tell me my soul?

Birds, fountains, winds and breezes, o let him sleep
    now, o let him sleep now,
Let him go on dreaming, dreaming and smiling.

Dodo, L'enfant Dors

SLEEP, BABY SLEEP

A lullaby reminiscent of the French lullaby but with its own distinctive character. *Belgian*

Dodo, l'enfant dors
L'enfant dormira bien vite.
Dodo, l'enfant dors
L'enfant dormira bientôt.
Dodo, l'enfant dors
L'enfant dormira bien vite.
Mm mm mm etc.

Sleep, baby sleep,
Baby go to sleep quite quickly.
Sleep, baby sleep,
Baby go to sleep at once.
Sleep, baby sleep,
Baby go to sleep quite quickly.
Mm Mm etc.

Nânez Binamêye Poyète

O SLEEP MY PRECIOUS CHICK

The provinces of Belgium embrace the Walloons, a people who speak a language closely related to French, which is one of the two spoken languages of Belgium. Wallonia has a rich folk culture and has contributed much to Belgium's musical history.

The soup mentioned is onion soup, but the English translation does not seem to leave room to include the type of soup!
Walloon

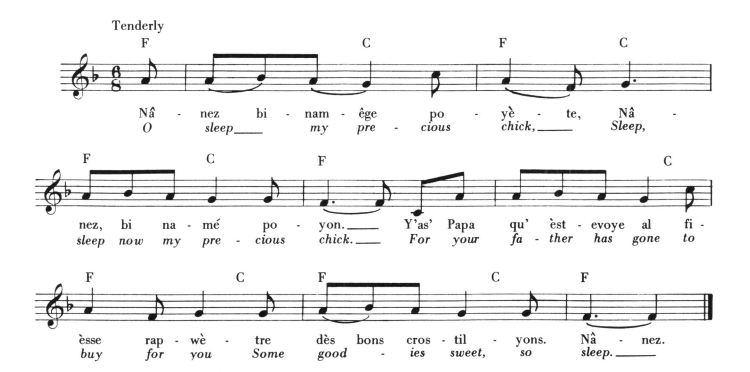

Nânez, binamêye poyète,
Nânez, binamé, poyon.
Y-a s'Papa qu'èst-evoye al fièsse,
Rapwètre dès bons crostilyons.
Nânez. . .

Nânez, binamêye poyète,
Nânez, binamé poyon.
Y-a s'mame qu'èst-evoye e pwèce,
Rapwètre dèl sope a lognon.
Nânez. . .

O sleep my precious chick,
Sleep, sleep, my precious chick.
For your father has gone to buy for you
Some goodies sweet, so sleep.

O sleep my precious chick,
Sleep, sleep, my precious chick.
For your mother has gone to church, and soon
She makes for you soup, so sleep.

Fi La Nanae, Mi Bel Fiole

HUSHABYE MY LITTLE BABE

This lullaby comes from Bologna Emilia and was collected by Dr. Maud Karpeles. Italian folk melodies were often accompanied by pipe or reed instruments and they have a very direct and somewhat earthy style. Here in spite of, or perhaps because of, its simplicity, the lullaby achieves a sense of drama and quite unexpected beauty as the melody rises to a climax and falls again. *Italian*

Fi la nanae mi bel fiol,
Fi la nanae mi bel fiol,
Fa si la nanna.
Dormi ben, e mi bel fiol.
Dormi ben, e mi bel fiol.
Fa si la nanna.

Hushabye my little babe,
Hushabye my little babe,
And sleep till daybreak.
Sweetly sleep my little babe,
Sweetly sleep my little babe,
Oh sleep till daybreak.

Ró Ró

This lullaby was recorded at Malhados (Miranda) and was sung by Justina de Jesus Igrejas. It comes from the province of Tras-os-Montes, which borders on Spain and is one of the most isolated parts of Portugal, and perhaps of Europe. In this province there are many areas which have their own dialect and Malhados is one of them. The first folk music collecting in this area was by Kurt Schindler, an American musicologist and composer.

The translator from the Portuguese Embassy pointed out that the literal translation in verse four is "the head of a donkey," and in verse five "the head of flame"; he suggested however that verse four could be translated in terms of stubbornness, and verse five in terms of an evil or flaming spirit, both of which prevented the child from going to sleep.

It is an enchanting lullaby with its infinitely patient "but not just yet." *Portuguese*

After the final verse repeat last three bars.

Cum róró pego no nino
Cum róró se vai dormindo.
O róró, o róró, qu'agora no.

Cum róró pego no nino
Cum róró se drumirá
O róró, o róró, qu'agora no.

E amanhana vou al molino,
Se me queres algo sal-me al camino
O róró, o róró, qu'agora no.

Vai-te dai, cabeca de burro,
Qu'al pai del nino aserva tudo.
O róró, o róró, qu'agora no.

Vai-te dai cabeça de lhama
Qu'el pai del nino ya está na cama
O róró, o róró, qu'agora no.

Anda dai, se queres benir,
Garra la capa e bamos,
Al camino, e ditosos
La capa yé de nos ambos.
O róró, o róró, qu'agora no.

Cum róró the little boy
Cum róró is going to sleep,
O róró, o róró, but not just yet.

Cum róró, the little boy
Cum róró, he will be sleeping,
O róró, o róró, but not just yet.

If you meet me at the windmill
You will find what you are wanting,
O róró, o róró, but not just yet.

Go away you stubborn spirit
For his father watches over him,
O róró, o róró, but not just yet.

Go away you flaming spirit
For his father now is sleeping,
O róró, o róró, but not just yet.

Let us go you want to sleep now,
Hold the cape and let's away,
On your way happily
Beneath our cape,
O róró, o róró, but not just yet.

ΚΟΙΜΑΤΑΙ ΤΟ ΜΩΡΟΥΤΣΚΟ ΜΟΥ

O SWEETLY DOES MY BABY SLEEP

The beauty of this lullaby lies in the use of chromatic intervals and the highly decorative melodic line which can be varied according to the whim of the singer; for it is said that no Greek folk song is sung the same way twice!

As Greece became the repository for Egyptian music, so at a later date Turkey became the repository for Greek music, and at the height of the Byzantine culture, Turkish songs embraced singing styles from all its surrounding peoples; hence the similarity between Turkish, Egyptian and Greek lullabies. *Greek*

Κοιμᾶται τὸ μωροῦτσκό μου
καὶ πῶς νά τό ᾽ξυπνήσω
νά πάρω διαμαντόπετραις,
νά τό πετροβολήσω.

Κοιμᾶται τὸ μωράκι μου
καὶ γὼ τὸ νανουρίζω
καὶ τὴν κουνίτσα του κουνῶ
καὶ τὸ γλυκογυρίζω.

Ἔλα, Χριστὲ καὶ Παναγιά,
καὶ πάρτε ᾽ς τῆς παξέδες
καὶ γιώμοστο τῆς κόρφαις του
λουλούδια μενεξέδες.

O sweetly does my baby sleep;
When he awakes from slumber deep,
Bright sparkling jewels I'll show him,
Gay coloured balls I'll throw him.

My baby in his cradle lies,
To him I sing sweet lullabies,
Gently his cradle I'm rocking,
Whilst o'er him I am watching.

O Virgin Mary, Mother of Christ,
Pour blessings on this babe of mine;
Fill his arms full of posies,
Sweet smelling herbs and roses.

Ela Ypne

COME SLEEP

This lullaby was sung to the author by Evangelia Paraskevopoulos, now living in Ottawa, Canada. She learnt it from
her mother, Lilika Dimitriadov.   *Greek*

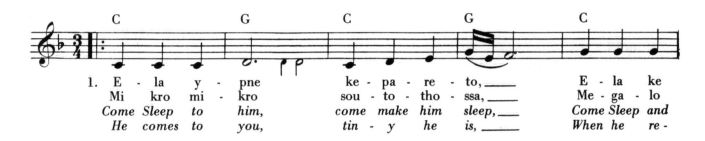

1. E - la y - pne   ke - pa - re - to,____   E - la ke   Me - ga - lo
   Mi kro mi - kro   sou - to - tho - ssa,____
   Come Sleep to him,   come make him sleep,____   Come Sleep and
   He comes to you,   tin - y he is,____   When he re -

ki - mi - sse mou to,____   O, o, o, o, o, o____
fe - le mou   to. ____
take   him, come make him sleep.
turns   he will be big.____

Ela, ypne, ke pare to,
Ela ke kimisse mou to,
Mikro-mikro sou tothossa,
Megalo fele mou to.

Refrain

Megalo ian psilo voeeno'
T'ssio san kyparissi
Ki kloné tou n'aplononte
T' Anatoli ' ke Dy'ssi.

Refrain

Come Sleep to him, come make him sleep,
Come Sleep and take him, come make him sleep.
He comes to you, tiny he is,
When he returns, he will be big.

Refrain

Big like a mountain, like a high mountain,
Straight as a cypress tree, straight and tall.
With all its branches, spreading and spreading,
The branches spread from east to west.

Refrain

Nam, Nam

A lullaby of rich imagination and deep feeling from a country with a long and fascinating history. Because of Malta's strategic position she has attracted many powerful nations to her shore. The Phoenicians were the earliest known rulers of the island and it is from them that the Maltese trace their origin and language. The Phoenicians were followed by Carthaginians, Romans, Arabs, Normans, Angevins, Aragonese and Castillians. Finally Malta was captured by the French under Napoleon Bonaparte and later passed to Britain in the year 1800.

This lullaby was noted by a well-known Maltese folklorist, Joseph Cassar Pullicino, and translated by Louis Grech. The translator said that the sore which the baby cannot forget is the kind of sore which occurs when a small child falls down in the dusty street and because of the dust picks up an infection. *Maltese*

Nam, nam,
Orqod, orqod, ibni orqod,
Qalb il-ward u l-gizimin,
Ghandex ommox il-madonna,
U nissierek il-bambin,
Nam, nam,

Orqod, orqod, ibni orqod,
Biex na ghttik fix-xuganan,
Ma, ghadni na nistax norqod
Ghax niftakar fil-musmar,
Nam, nam.

Nam, nam,
Sleep, sleep, little child,
'Neath the roses and the jasmine,
Your mother is the Madonna,
And your father's the child Jesus.
Nam, nam.

Sleep, sleep, little child,
I will cover you with bedclothes,
"Mother, I still cannot sleep,
For I can't forget my sore."
Nam, nam.

Central & Eastern Europe

Aija Anzit Aija — *Latvian*
Močiute Mano — *Lithuanian*
Hej Pada Pada Rosiçka — *Slovakian*
Aludj Baba, Aludjál — *Hungarian*
Unsij, Unsij — *Polish*

Aija Anzit Aija

GO TO SLEEP MY JAMIE

This country no longer has a separate identity, but its folk songs, which are many and beautiful, are Latvian and as such they remind the people of the rich cultural heritage of their past. *Latvian*

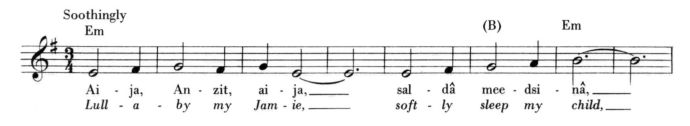

Ai - ja, An - zit, ai - ja,___ sal - dâ mee - dsi - nâ,___
Lull - a - by my Jam - ie,___ soft - ly sleep my child,___

Mah - sin te - wi schuh - pos,___ Weeg - lam ro - zi - nam.___
Sis - ter rocks you gen - tly,___ Soft her hands and mild.___

Aija, Anzit, aija,
Saldâ meedsinâ,
Mahsin tewi schuhpos
Weeglam roziņam.

Augs trejadas awis,
Manam Anzischam,
Strupj-un garastites,
Sprogainites ar!

Trejeem sirgeem brauza
Tawâs Krustibâs.
Deews dod Anzischami
Sescheem sirgeem braukt.

Lullaby my Jamie,
Softly sleep my child,
Sister rocks you gently;
Soft her hands and mild.

Snow white lambs for Jamie,
Every kind your own,
Curly, bobtailed, longtailed,
When a man you've grown.

To your christening, three steeds
We drove all the way.
God grant six fine horses
You may drive some day.

Močiute Mano

MOTHER, DEAREST MOTHER

This country too has no separate identity, but its folk songs are still cherished. The lullaby is a dialogue between the restless little girl who cannot sleep, and her mother who tries to comfort her. The melody, which only uses four notes, reminds one of the play songs that children make up and pass on to each other. *Lithuanian*

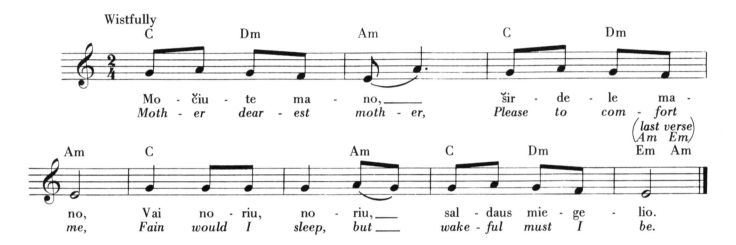

Mo - čiu - te ma - no,_____ šir - de - le ma -
Moth - er dear - est moth - er, Please to com - fort

no, Vai no - riu, no - riu,___ sal - daus mie - ge - lio.
me, Fain would I sleep, but ___ wake - ful must I be.

Močiute mano, širdele mano,
Vai noriu, noriu, saldaus miegelio.

Dukrele mano, jaunoji mano,
Eik; darželi, pas lelijěles.

Vėjalis putě, lelijos linko,
Tai tu dukrele saldžia miegosi.

Mother, dearest mother,
Please to comfort me,
Fain would I sleep,
But wakeful must I be.

Daughter, dearest daughter,
Pray come close to me,
There in the garden,
Lilies you will see.

Gently the lilies,
Swaying in the breeze,
You too shall sleep,
As the wind will bring you ease.

Hej Pada Pada Rosiçka

SLUMBER SLUMBER ROSIÇKA

This lullaby is very well known and its words vary from place to place. Sometimes it is sung in a very sad way, at other times it can sound happy, but always the suggestive repetitive words court sleep. It can be sung as a round, and as such the whole family can help to put baby to sleep!

Slovakia no longer exists as a separate country, but Slovaks keep their own language and as part of Czechoslovakia they have contributed to the marvelously rich folk heritage. When a nation has to fight to survive, folk music plays a vital role, both as a method of communication and as a method of preserving the traditions of their culture. The Czech language is a language rich in diminutives, which lends itself to the singing of lullabies. *Slovakian*

Hej pada pada Rosiçka,
Spaly by moje Rosiçka,
Spaly by moje, spaly by aj tvoje.
Spaly by dusa moja oboje,
Spaly by moje, spaly by aj tvoje,
Spaly by dusa moja oboje.

Slumber, slumber Rosiçka,*
Slumber, slumber Rosiçka,
I am so sleepy, you too are sleepy,
We are so sleepy, both of us.
I am so sleepy, you too are sleepy,
We are so sleepy, both of us.

*Rosicka is a term of endearment, and as such it needs no translation. It is something like "little rose," but used in the way that the French would say "little cabbage," or in the way that in Canada or England one might say "honey."

Aludj Baba, Aludjál

O SLUMBER LITTLE BABY

The Magyars of Hungary had their own musical styles, songs, scales and modes; much of this individual character has been made known to the world by the writings and compositions of Zoltán Kodály and Béla Bartók, who made full use of the folk music heritage of their country. The wild gypsy character has influenced their music and is particularly noticeable in their folk music. They have an intense love of their country and this again is reflected in their lullabies. *Hungarian*

Very smoothly

A - ludj ba - ba, a - lud - jál, Le - szállt már a csil - lag.
O slum - ber lit - tle ba - by. The stars have all van - ished.

Csön - get - tyüs kis fe - hér bá - rány, Ha - za fe - lé ba - lag. Fész-
Lit - tle lamb with tink - ling bell is slow - ly head - ing home - wards. The

ké - re szállt - az er - dön, A da - los ma - dár - ka,
ti - ny sing - ing bird has flown home to her nest. Our

Do - rom - bo - ló ci - cánk is fel - ült a pat - ká - ra. A-
pus - sy cat has set - tled down be - side the warm fire - place. O

ludj ba - ba, a - lud - jál, Le - szállt már a csil - lag
slum - ber lit - tle ba - by, The stars have all van - ished.

Csön - get - tyüs kis fe - hér bá - rány Ha - za - fe - lé ba - leag.
Lit - tle lamb with tink - ling bell is slow - ly head - ing home - wards.

A-ludj ba-ba, a-lud-jál,
Le-szállt már a csi-lag
Csön-get-tyüs kis fe-hér bá-rány
Ha-za-fe-lé bal-lag.
Fész-ké-re szállt az er-dőn,
A da-los ma-dár-ka,
Do-rom-bo-ló ci-cánk is fel-ült a pat-ká-ra.
A-ludj ba-ba, a-lud-jál,
Le-szállt már a csil-lag,
Csön-get-tyüs kis fe-hér bá-rány
Ha-za-fe-lé bal-lag.

O slumber little baby,
The stars have all vanished.
Little lamb with tinkling bell
Is slowly heading homewards.
The tiny singing bird
Has flown home to her nest.
Our pussy cat has settled down
Beside the warm fireplace.
O slumber little baby,
The stars have all vanished.
Little lamb with tinkling bell
Is slowly heading homewards.

Unsij, Unsij

SLEEP, SLEEP

A rather sad little lullaby in which baby is told that the sky is darkening, and alas, the gypsies have stolen his pillows!
Polish

At a moderate pace, wistfully

1. Us - nij, ze mi us - nij, Mo - je ma - le us - nij,
Fall a - sleep, a - sleep now, Ba - by fall a - sleep now,

Mo - je ma - lu - sien - kie, Si - we, si - wiu - ten - kie,
Ba - by fall a - sleep now, As the sky grows grey now,

Mo - je ma - lu - sien - kje, Si - we, si - win - ten - kie.
Ba - by fall a - sleep,___ As the sky grows grey - er.

Usnij, ze mi usnij,	*Fall asleep, asleep now,*
Moje male usnij,	*Baby fall asleep now,*
Moje malusien kie,	*Baby fall asleep now,*
Siwe, siwiutenkie	*As the sky grows grey now,*
Moje malusjenkie	*Baby fall asleep,*
Siwe, siwiutenkie.	*As the sky grows greyer.*
Usnij, ze mi usnij,	*Fall asleep, asleep now,*
Choc na gote ziemi,	*Though the ground is barren*
Bo ci cyganeczki	*For the gypsy girls have*
Poduszeczki wzigli.	*Stolen all your pillows,*
Bo ci cyganeczki	*For the gypsy girls have*
Poduszeczki wzigli.	*Stolen all your pillows.*

Latin America

Duérmete Mi Niño — *Mexican*
A La Rorro Niño — *Guatemalan*
Dormite Niñito — *El Salvador*
Dormite Niñito — *Honduras*
Duérmete Niño Chiquito — *Venezuelan*
Duerme Niño Pequeñito — *Colombian*
Rouxinol Do Pico Preto — *Brazilian*
Arroro Mi Niño — *Argentinian*

Duérmete Mi Niño

SLEEP MY LITTLE BABY

Mexican folk songs combine Indian and Spanish elements, and it is not easy to distinguish between the two cultures. The Indian elements are part of the Aztec and Mayan culture when Aztec was the spoken language. Many Aztec writings are preserved although Spanish is now the spoken language. The folk songs are still part of Mexican every day life and they show the same enthusiasm for their music as they do for their children and their flowers. *Mexican*

Duérmete mi niño,
Duér - me - te so - li - to,
Sleep my lit - tle ba - by sleep - ing now so lone - ly,

Qué cuan - do te des - pier - tes,
Te doy at - ol - i - to.
But when you a - wak - en, Pret - ty toys will greet you.

Duérmete mi niño
Duérmete solito,
Qué cuando te despiertes,
Te doy atolito.

Sleep my little baby,
Sleeping now so lonely,
But when you awaken
Pretty toys will greet you.

A La Rorro Niño

LULLABY MY BABY

Guatemala is the most northerly state of Central America. It has a large Indian population, but musically the Spanish influence predominates. *Guatemalan*

A la ror - ro ni - ño, A la ro - ro ro,_____
Lull - la - by my ba -- by, Lul - la lul - la - by,_____

Duér - me - te mi niño,_____ Duér - me - te mi a - mor._____
Go to sleep my ba - by,___ Go to sleep my love._____

A la rorro niño,
A la rororo,
Duérmete mi niño,
Duérmete mi amor.

Lullaby my baby
Lulla lullaby,
Go to sleep my baby,
Go to sleep my love.

Dormite Niñito

NOW SLEEP LITTLE BABY

El Salvador is a country which in the past provided a rich hunting ground for the Spanish in gold and silver and some precious stones. The lullaby, with its references to silver and diamonds, may reflect a looking back on the part of the mother to the time when their excellent gold and silver craftsmen were much in demand.   *El Salvador*

Dor - mi - te ni - ñi - to,   no llo - res chi - qui - to,
Now sleep lit - tle ba - by,   don't cry lit - tle dar - ling,

Ven - drán an - gel - li - tos   las som - bras de no - che.
The an - gels are com - ing   with shad - ows of ev - ening.

Ray - i - tos de lu - na   ray - i - tos de pla - ta,
The rays of the moon - light   spin fine threads of sil - ver,

A - lum bran a mi ni - ño,   que es - tá en la cu - na.
To shine on my ba - by,   a - sleep in his cra - dle.

Ray - i - tos del sol,   el cie - lo a - zul,
The rays of the sun,   the blue of the sky,

De - jan   de dor - mir   y_em - pie - zan a vi - vir.
Will wake   him from   dreams   when morn - ing is   nigh.

Dor - mi - te ni - ñi - to,   con o - jos de dia - man - tes,
Now sleep lit - tle   ba - by,   with eyes bright as   dia - monds,

Es - tre - llas bri - llan - tes,   flo - ri - do el   cie - lo.
And bril - liant as   star - light   that shines from the heav - ens.

Dormite niñito no llores chiquito,
Vendrán angelitos, las sombras de noche.
Rayitos de luna, rayitos de plata,
Alumbran a mi niño, que está en la cuna.
Rayitos del sol, el cielo azul,
Dejan de dormir, y empiezan a vivir.
Dormite niñito, con ojos de diamantes,
Estrellas brillantes, florido el cielo.

Now sleep little baby, don't cry little darling,
The angels are coming with shadows of evening.
The rays of the moonlight spin fine threads of silver,
To shine on my baby, asleep in his cradle.
The rays of the sun, the blue of the sky,
Will wake him from dreams when morning is nigh.
Now sleep little baby, with eyes bright as diamonds,
And brilliant as starlight that shines from the heavens.

Dormite Niñito

SLEEP LITTLE ONE

Honduras, probably the most isolated of the states contributes a simple but charming lullaby, also predominantly Spanish. *Honduras*

Very smoothly

Dor - mi - te ni - ñi - to que ten - go que ha - cer,
Sleep___ lit - tle one I have some - thing to do,

Lav - ar tus pañ - al - es, sen - tar - me a co - ser.
I must wash your pant - ies, sit me down to sew.

Dor - mi - te ni - ñi - to, ca - be - za de ay - o - te,
Sleep___ lit - tle one, sleep my lit - tle sleep - y head,

Si no te dor - mis, te co - me el coy - o - te.
If you do not sleep, coy - otes will___ eat you.

La Vir - gen la - va - ba Don Jo - se ten - dí - a,
Ma - ry moth - er washed, St. Jos - eph spread the clothes,

El Ni - ño llor - a - ba del frí - o que ha - cia
While the Christ child cried from the bit - ter cold.

Ar -

90

ru, ar - ru - rú.   ar - ru,   ar - ru - rú,   Ar -

ru,   ar - ru - rú,   ar - ru - rú, ___   ar - ru - rú.

Dormite niñito que tengo que hacer,
Lavar tus pañales, sentarme a coser.
Dormite niñito, cabeza de ayote,
Si no te dormis, te come el coyote.
La Virgen lavaba, Don Jose tendía,
El Niño lloraba del frío que hacia.
Ar-ru, ar-ru-rú, ar-ru, ar-ru-rú,
Ar-ru, ar-ru-rú, ar-ru-rú, ar-ru-rú.

Sleep little one I have something to do,
I must wash your panties, sit me down to sew.
*Sleep little one, sleep my little sleepy head,**
If you do not sleep, the coyote will eat you.
Mother Mary washed, St. Joseph spread the clothes,
While the Christ child cried from the bitter cold.
Ar-ru, ar-ru-rú, ar-ru, ar-ru-rú,
Ar-ru, ar-ru-rú, ar-ru-rú, ar-ru-rú.

---

*
My little sleepy head might be my little pumpkin head in North America,
and my little cabbage in France, so any appropriate term can be used.

Duérmete Niño Chiquito

GO TO SLEEP MY LITTLE DARLING

Venezuela has a long tradition of folk song and dance. It is said that musically the Negro influence is paramount in the coastal regions, Indian in the plains, and Spanish in the cities. The guava mentioned in the lullaby is a delicious fruit which flourishes in tropical climates.   *Venezuelan*

Duérmete niño chiquito
Que tu madre está aquí,
Que se fué a buscar guayabas
Las mejores para tí.

Si este niño no se duerme,
Que noche pasaré yo!
Pasaré la noche en vela,
Cantándole el arrorró.

Go to sleep my little darling
For your mother is not here,
She has gone to get the guavas
Quite the best of fruits for you.

If you do not go to sleep
What a night it will be!
I will have to stay awake
Singing lullabies to thee.

Duerme Niño Pequeñito

SLEEP MY BABY, LITTLE DARLING

In Colombian folk music there is the same blending of
Indian, Negro and Spanish elements. *Colombian*

Duer-me niño,— pequ-ue-ñi-to, Que la no-che vie-ne ya,
Sleep my ba-by, lit-tle dar-ling, For the night is draw-ing nigh,

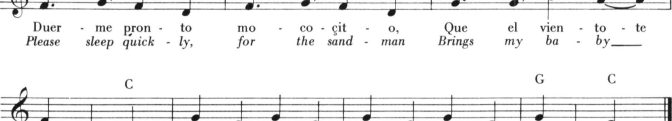

Duer-me pron-to mo-co-çit-o, Que el vien-to-te
Please sleep quick-ly, for the sand-man Brings my ba-by____

arul-la-rá. Mm mm mm mm Mm mm mm mm mm— mm.
lul-la-by.

Duerme niño, pequeñito,
Que la noche viene ya,
Duerme pronto mococito,
Que el vientote arullará.
Mm . . . etc.

Sleep my baby, little darling,
For the night is drawing nigh,
Please sleep quickly, for the sandman
Brings my baby lullaby.
Mm Mm etc.

Rouxinol Do Pico Preto

NIGHTINGALE WITH THE BLACK BEAK

Brazil is an enormous state which covers nearly half of South America. The people speak Portuguese, and although many of their folk songs are sung in Spanish, there are also many specifically Portuguese folk songs. The music has great vitality, and Villa Lobos has used many of the folk melodies in his compositions. *Brazilian*

Mournfully

Roux - in - ol do pic - o pre - to, Roux - in - ol do pic - o pre - to, De - i - xa a ba - ga do lou - eir - o. o o. o o o o
Night - in - gale with the black beak, Night - in - gale with the black beak, Leave the fruit of the laur - el tree.

Rouxinol do pico preto,
Rouxinol do pico preto,
Deixa a baga do loueiro.
O, O!

Deixa dormir o menino,
Deixa dormir o menino,
Que stá no sono primeiro.
O, O!

Dorme, dorme, meu menino,
Dorme, dorme, meu menino,
Que a maezinha logo vem.
O, O!

Foi lavar os cueirinhos,
Foi lavar os cueirinhos,
A ribeira de Belém.
O, O!

Nightingale with the black beak,
Nightingale with the black beak,
Leave the fruit of the laurel tree.
O! O!

Leave the baby to sleep,
Leave the baby to sleep,
He is in his first good sleep.
O! O!

Sleep, oh sleep my baby,
Sleep, oh sleep my baby,
Your mother will come soon.
O! O!

She has gone to wash your panties,
She has gone to wash your panties,
On the banks of Belém.
O! O!

Arroro Mi Niño

LULLABY MY BABY

Argentina is the home of the gaucho, the equivalent of
the American cowboy. It is the largest of the Spanish speaking
states and one of the richest as its name, derived from the Latin
for silver, implies. *Argentinian*

Plaintively

Ar - ro - ro mi ni - ño, Ar - ro - ro mi sol,
Lul - la - by my ba - by, Lul - la - by my sun,

Ar - ro - ro pe - da - zo, de mi cor - a - zón.
Sleep my heart's own trea - sure, moth - er's lit - tle one.

Duér - me - te mi ni - ño, Ten - go qué hac - er,
Go to sleep my ba - by Time so quick - ly goes,

La - var los pañ - al - es Plan - char - y co - cer.
I must wash your pant - ies, starch and iron your clothes.

Verse 3 repeats the music of verse 2.

Arroro mi niño,	*Lullaby my baby,*
Arroro mi sol,	*Lullaby my sun,*
Arroro pedazo,	*Sleep my heart's own treasure,*
De mi corazón.	*Mother's little one.*
Duérmete mi niño,	*Go to sleep my baby,*
Tengo qué hacer,	*Time so quickly goes.*
Lavar los pañales	*I must wash your panties,*
Planchar y cocer.	*Starch and iron your clothes.*
Este niño lindo,	*Yes, my pretty baby*
Se quiere dormier,	*Wants no more to play,*
Y el pícaro, sueño,	*But the prankish Sandman*
No quiere venir.	*Will not come his way.*

Africa

Sleep My Baby — *Nigerian*
Yeke Omo Mi — *Nigerian*
Congo Lullaby — *Congolese*

Sleep My Baby

Another lullaby with its pattern of drumming.   *Nigerian*

Sleep my baby near to me,
Lu lu lu, lu lu lu, close your vel-vet eyes.
Far a-way in their nest ba-by birds flut-ter down to rest,— High in the trees, far from harm, ti-ny mon-key sleeps— Deep in his moth-er's arms.—

Sleep my baby near to me,
Lu, lu, lu, lu, lu, lu,
Close your velvet eyes.
Far away in their nest

Baby birds flutter down to rest,
High in the trees far from harm
Tiny monkey sleeps
Deep in his mother's arms.

Yeke Omo Mi

SLUMBER SONG

The pattern of drumming in this lullaby is as much a part of the song as the words. The rhythmic pattern in this lullaby is known as Omele and belongs to the Yorube speaking people, but is is popular with all Nigerians.

The translation of this lullaby is by Holsaert-Bailey.
Nigerian

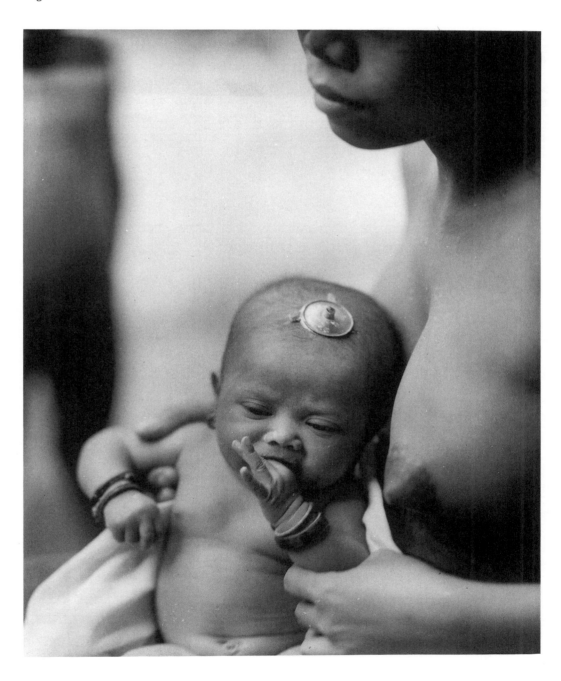

Guitar, single sweeping strums on the beat, or follow the drum/clapping rhythm.

Ye-ke omo mi, omo mi yeke,
Yeke omo mi, omo mi yeke.
Emi ni iyare, yeke omo mi
Omo mi yeke emi ni iyare,
Yeke omo mi, omo mi yeke.
Epe bomi omo, gege birawo
Tipe b'o supa, oto, omo mi, omo mi oto.

Oh do not cry, my little treasure,
Oh do not cry, my little treasure,
For here is your mother.
Oh do not cry, my little loved one,
For here is your mother.
Oh do not cry, my little treasure.
Dear children yonder strewn,
Around us come soon
Like stars round the moon.
Oh do not cry, my little loved one.

Oto omo mi, omo mi oto
Oto omo mi, omo mi oto
Emi ni babare, oto omo mi
Omo mi oto emi ni babare
Oto omo mi, omo mi oto.
Epe bomi omo, gege birawo
Tipe b'o supa, oto, omo mi, omo mi oto.

Oh hushabye, my little treasure,
Oh hushabye, my little treasure,
For here is your father.
Oh hushabye, my little loved one,
For here is your father.
Oh hushabye, my little treasure.
Dear children yonder strewn,
Around us come soon
Like stars round the moon.
Oh do not cry, my little loved one.

Congo Lullaby

This simple lullaby uses a rudimentary pentatonic scale.
Congolese

Guitar: Try a single strum followed by a tap on the guitar body, or simply the steady tap on its own.

Yo, yo, yo, yo, yo,
Yo, yo, yo, yo, yo.
Mwana (baby) dear now do not cry,
Soon will come your ta-ta (father)
Food he'll bring you by and by,
And perhaps a ba-ta (duck).
Yo, yo, yo, yo, yo,
Yo, yo, yo, yo, yo.

Asia

Hawa Dheray Aana

ROCKING, ROCKING TO REST

This beautiful lullaby with its haunting melody and equally lovely words was sung to the authors by Kailash Anand, of Montreal, who sang it to her children. Her husband translated the Indian words and was satisfied with the way they were adapted to fit the music. The English does not follow the Indian words exactly, as far as the order of the words in the song are concerned; however, the ideas and meanings of the words are not changed. *Indian*

Humming

Nin - de bhar - ay   Pan - kh - le - yay   jh - olla, jh - ula jaa - na
O whis-p'ring breeze, sway   her to sleep, with thy sleep - la - den__ wings,

Nin - de bhar - ay   Pan - kh - le - yay   jh - olla,__ jh - ula jaa - na
O whis-p'ring breeze, sway her to sleep, with thy__ sleep la - den wings.

Nan - hi kal - i   son - ay cha - li   ha - wa Dher - ay   aa - na.__
This ti - ny bud drow - si - ly sleeps, Rock-ing, rock-ing to rest.

Nin - de bhar - ay   pan - kh - le - yay.__   Chand ki - ran - see   gur - i - a - h
O whis-p'ring breeze sway her to sleep.__   This babe so frail, as moon-light pale,

ma - jon ki - hay pa - li ___ Chand ki - ran - see gur - i - a - h
reared with spoil - ing love. This babe so frail, as moon-light pale,

ma - jon ki - hay pa - li Aaj ___ a - gar ch - and - ni ___ aa
reared with spoil - ing love. O moon-light shine, on this child of mine,

aa ___ na ___ me - ri ga - li ___ Gun gun gun, geet ko - i
lull her, lull her to sleep. Silk - en cords do no harm

ho - lay ___ ho - lay ___ gaa - na. ___ Nin - de bhar - ay pan - kh le - yay
tan - gled ___ with ti - ny feet. ___ O whis-p'ring breeze, sway her to sleep,

jh-oola, jh - ula jaa - na. Humming
with thy sleep la - den ___ wings.

Ray - sham ki - doar a - gar par - on ko ___ ul - j hay
If my prin - cess should a - wake up soothe her, soothe her to sleep

Ray - sham ki - doar a - gar par on ko ___ ul - j hay
If my prin - cess should wa - ken up Soothe her, soothe her to sleep.

Ghoon - gar ka - da - na kol shoar macha joy Ra - ni mee - ri ja ___ gay
Swing high her nest with your soft wings Lull her lull her to ___ sleep,

To - phir nin - d ya tu bah la - na___
Tink - ling bells cause no a-larm with your___ mu-sic___ sweet,

Nin - de bhar - ay pan - kh le - yay jh-oola jh - ula jaa - na
O whis-p'ring breeze sway her to sleep With thy sleep la - den wings,

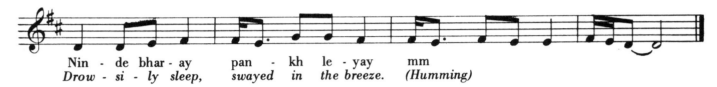

Nin - de bhar - ay pan - kh le - yay mm
Drow - si - ly sleep, swayed in the breeze. (Humming)

Chords in brackets cover the 2 parts of the melody. Accompaniment, if at all, should be very unobtrusive.

Ninde bharay pankh leyay jholla jhula jaana
Ninde bharay pankh leyay jholla jhula jaana
Nanhi kali sonay chali hawa dheray aana.
Ninde bharay pankh leyay.

Chand kiran see guriah majon ki hay pali
Chand kiran see guriah majon ki hay pali
Aaj agar chandni aa aana meri gali
Gun gun gun, geet koi holay holay gaana
Ninde bharay pankh leyay jholla jhula jaana

Raysham ki doar agar paron ko uljhay
Raysham ki doar agar paron ko uljhay
Ghoongar ka dana koi shoar macha joy
Rani meeri jagay to phir nindya tu bahlana
Ninde bharay pankh leyay jhoola jhula jaana
Ninde bharay pankh leyay.

O whisp'ring breeze, sway her to sleep,
With thy sleep laden wings,
O whisp'ring breeze, sway her to sleep,
With thy sleep laden wings.
This tiny bud drowsily sleeps,
Rocking, rocking to rest.
O whisp'ring breeze, sway her to sleep.

This babe so frail, as moonlight pale,
Reared with spoiling love,
This babe so frail, as moonlight pale,
Reared with spoiling love,
O moonlight shine on this child of mine,
Lull her, lull her, to sleep.
Silken cords do no harm, tangled with tiny feet,
O whisp'ring breeze, sway her to sleep,
With thy sleep laden wings.

If my princess should wake up
Soothe her, soothe her to sleep,
If my princess should wake up
Soothe her, soothe her to sleep.
Swing high her nest with your soft wings,
Lull her, lull her to sleep,
Tink'ling bells cause no alarm with your music sweet,
O whisp'ring breeze, sway her to sleep,
With thy sleep laden wings,
Drowsily sleep, swayed in the breeze ---

Ninni Baba

COME NOW, SLEEP

A simple lullaby chant in great contrast to "Hawa Dheray Aana." *Indian*

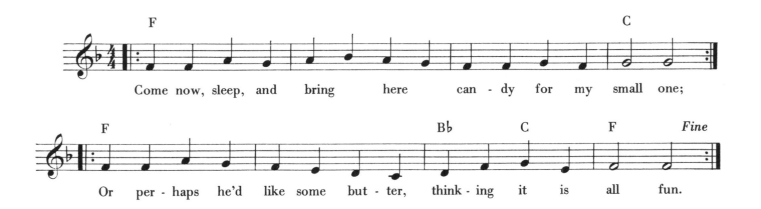

Come now, sleep, and bring here can - dy for my small one;

Or per - haps he'd like some but - ter, think - ing it is all fun.

Come now, sleep, and bring here candy for my small
  one;
Or perhaps he'd like some butter, thinking it is all fun.

I am coming, ho! hum! but I visit others,
When they sleep, I'll rock your cradle as I did your
  mother's.

The Bamboo Flute

According to an ancient Chinese custom, on the child's first birthday, gifts are placed at random on a table in front of the baby; whatever he reaches for first is supposed to indicate his choice of a profession. These gifts include such items as a pen for a writer, a flute for a musician and so on. This lullaby probably indicates that baby has chosen a flute and is destined to be a musician. On the other hand the flute is a popular instrument and may merely be used as one method of putting baby to sleep.

The melody, which is a folk melody, is based on the pentatonic scale, and the translation of the words is by Evelyn Modoi. *Chinese*

From the bamboo mother makes a flute,
Bamboo flute for baby small.
Held in little hands,
Pressed to rosy lips,
Lilting melodies rise and fall.
Lu lu lu lu, melodies rise and fall.
Lu lu lu lu, sleepy heads nod and fall.

Three Sinhalese Lullabies

This chant has a number of alternate rhythms and they are selected according to which words are being sung.

The three verses given here were collected and translated by Mrs. Nimal Perere, an authority on Sinhalese lullabies.
Sinhalese

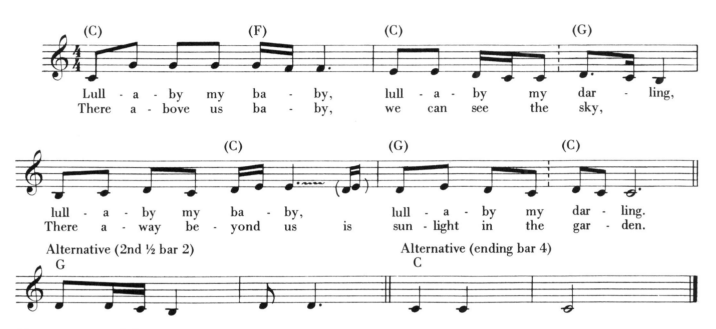

Lull - a - by my ba - by, lull - a - by my dar - ling,
There a - bove us ba - by, we can see the sky,

lull - a - by my ba - by, lull - a - by my dar - ling.
There a - way be - yond us is sun - light in the gar - den.

Alternative (2nd ½ bar 2)

Alternative (ending bar 4)

Best unaccompanied.

Lullaby my baby, lullaby my darling,
Lullaby my baby, lullaby my darling.
There above us baby, we can see the sky,
There away beyond us, is sunlight in the garden.

Lullaby my baby, lullaby my darling,
Lullaby my baby, lullaby my darling.
Where my little one has your mother gone?
She goes to the pond where blue lilies grow.

Lullaby my baby, lullaby my darling,
Lullaby my baby, lullaby my darling.
When at night my son, clouds come o'er the moon,
Then it's time my son, to sleep and cease to cry.

Slumber Song

This lullaby was collected and arranged by Saranagupta Amarasinha, one of the most distinguished of Ceylon's singers. He has collected and set Sinhalese folk songs to the western system of notation, thus making them available to a wider public. In Ceylon he is well known for his interest in furthering the cause of Sinhalese music.   *Sinhalese*

At a moderate pace

Refrain

Tho-i Tho-i___ Thoi___ Tho-i ye pu-thā___
Sleep, sleep,___ sleep,___ sleep my___ son,___

ba-i ba-i ba-i___ ba-i ye pu-thā___ babá magā
Rest, rest,___ rest, rest my___ son.___ My ba-by

hon The ha pe nà Thave sete ko-lem___
is a cle-ver___ lit-tle one Each day he will go___

bete ya ne và___ pa nam thi ha k padi ka ne
to Col-ombo cit-y Thir-ty pan-anas he earns ev-er-y

và i-n pa ne-m ak___ ma te Thenne và___
day, and to me he gives one of___ these.___

Tho-i, tho-i, tho-i, tho-i ye pu-thā
Ba-i, ba-i, ba-i, ba-i ye pu-thā
Babá magá hon THe ha pe nā
THave sete ko lem bete ya ne và
Pa nam thi ha k padi ka ne và
I-n pa ne-m ak ma te THenne và.

Sleep, sleep, sleep, sleep my son,
Rest, rest, rest, rest my son.
My baby is a clever little one
Each day he will go to Colombo city,
Thirty pananas he earns every day,
And to me he gives one of these.

Tho-i, tho-i, tho-i, tho-i ye pu-thā
Ba-i, ba-i, ba-i, ba-i ye pu-thā
Onne babo átninniyá
Gal ar-m-bā si-tin-niyá
Galin galete paninniyá
Babu Thäkelá THuvannilyá

Sleep, sleep, sleep, sleep my son,
Rest, rest, rest, rest my son.
Here my baby is a she elephant,
She sits on a big heap, big heap of rocks,
She can spring to one rock, then to another,
Seeing you my baby she runs away.

Tho-i, tho-i, tho-i, tho-i ye pu-thā
Ba-i, ba-i, ba-i, ba-i ye pu-thā
Ti-ki-ri, ti-ki-ri, ti-ki-ri liyá
Kàleth aran linTH ete giyá
LinTHe vatekere kaberegoyá
Kakule kàpi Thiyebariy-á.

Sleep, sleep, sleep, sleep my son,
Rest, rest, rest, rest my son.
A small little sweet darling girl
Took her pot for water, went to the well.
Round and round the well went iguana
And a diyabariya bit her throat.

Komoriuta

LULLABY

This lullaby, to judge by the many different arrangements available, is perhaps the best known of the Japanese lullabies. It is a very old lullaby and the version selected here is by Shuichi Taugawa with an English translation by Tamako Nina.   *Japanese*

Nen - ne - n   yo; _____   o - ko - ro - ri - yo!
Sleep,   go   to   sleep my   ba - by.   Close your   lit - tle   eyes.

Bo - ya - wa _   yoi _ ko - do   nen - ne - shi - na.
My   boy   is   a   good _ ba - by,   sleep   ba - by   sleep.

Nen-nen yo, okororoye.
Boyawa yoikoda, nen neshina.

Neyano omiyage nani morata
Denden taikoni she ne fue.

Sleep, go to sleep my baby,
Close your little eyes.
My boy is a good baby,
Sleep, baby sleep.

What will be brought to baby
From yonder town?
A lovely flute, and a
Deep sounding drum.

Lullaby

This lullaby is very simple and forms a great contrast to the Indian lullaby. Kashmir is a mountainous and wild country, which apart from some Islamic infiltration has been somewhat isolated musically. *Kashmiri*

Drink thy milk, Leav-ing none in the cup.

Then, my lisp-ing one, Go then to sleep.

This is better with no accompaniment.

Drink thy milk,
Leaving none in the cup.
Then, my lisping one,
Go then to sleep.

Jewish

Lulla Lulla Lullaby
Ayle Lyule
Zolst Azoy Lebn Un Zayn Gezint
Rozinkes Mit Mandlen

Lulla Lulla Lullaby

This lullaby, which is a beautiful little lullaby in the true folk tradition, comes directly from Israel; a "home grown" lullaby, sung at home, instead of a lullaby remembered over the years but sung in exile. *Jewish*

Lulla lulla lullaby,
Sleep my little girl,
Lulla lulla lullaby,
Sleep child well for me.
Your father left for work today,
He will return,

And he will bring a gift for you
When shines the moon.
Lulla lulla lullaby,
Sleep my little girl,
Lulla lulla lullaby,
Sleep my child for mother.

Ayle Lyule

AYLI LULI LULI

This traditional lullaby shows how the working mother supports her men folk (sons and husbands) so that they may become scholars and pious men. This achievement is one that raises the status of the family, including, of course, that of the working mother. *Jewish*

Ay lye lyu lye lyu lye
Shiof-zhe shiof mayn g'dule,
Mach-zhe tsu dayne
Eygelech di fayne.

Un shtey oyf vider,
Mit gezunte glider,
Mayn lib-zis kind,
Gich un geshvind.

In mark vei ich loyfin,
Beygelech vel ich koyfn,
Mit puter vel ich shmirn,
Tsu der chupe zol ich dich firn.

Vest oysvaksn a groysinker,
Vestu zayn a tane!
Vein dich ale
Zayn mich mekane!

Ayli lu li, lu li.
Sleep my precious baby,
Close your pretty eyes,
Close your lovely eyes.

When you wake up by and by,
You'll be healthy, you'll be spry,
Now you must go to sleep,
Now you must go to sleep.

I will hurry home from the square,
Get some fresh rolls for you there,
I'll butter them for you,
Find a sweet bride for you too.

You'll be a scholar of renown,
The wisest man in all the town,
For your piety,
Every one will envy me!

Zolst Azoy Lebn Un Zayn Gezint

I'LL SING TO YOUR BABY, IT WON'T CRY

One of the few lullabies attributed to a baby sitter, with English words by Ruth Rubin, who collected the last stanza. The baby sitter was a little girl of not more than ten years of age. *Jewish*

Zolst a-zoy le-bn un, zayn ge-zint, Vi ich __ vel dir zit-sn un vi-gn dos kind. Ay -lyu __ -lyu __ sha - sha - sha, Di ma - me iz ge gang - en in mark a - ayn. Ay - lyll - lyll, _____ shlof mayn kind, Di ma - me-shi vet ku - men gich un gesh - vind.

I'll sing to your ba - by, It won't cry, I'll wait till you come home, by and by. Hush lit - tle ba - by Don't you cry your mom - my will come home by and by: Sleep lit - tle ba - by, I'll sing you a song, Your mom-my will come home, she won't be long.

Zolst azoy lebn un zayn gezint
Vi ich vel dir zitsn un vign dos kind.
Ay-lyu-lyu, sha-sha-sha
Di mame iz gegangen in mark aayn.
Ay-lyu-lyu, shlof mayn kind,
Di mameshi vet kumen gich un geshvind.

Refrain

Andere meydelech tantsn un shpringen,
Un ich darf dem kind lidelech zingen.

Andere meydelech tsukerkelech nashn,
Un ich darf dem kind's vindelech vashn.

Dayn mame iz a tshatshke aza yor af ir,
Az du shlofst nit ayn, shrayt zi af mir.

*I'll sing to your baby, it won't cry,
I'll wait till you come home, by and by.
Hush little baby, don't you cry,
Your mommy will come home by and by.
Sleep little baby, I'll sing you a song,
Your mommy will return, she won't be long.*

Refrain

*Other little girls can romp and play,
But I must sing to baby all the day.*

*While other little girls eat sugar candies
Your mother makes me scrub your dirty panties.*

*Your mother's a mean one, this I know,
If you don't go to sleep, she'll scold me so!*

Rozinkes Mit Mandlen

RAISINS AND ALMONDS

Here is a lullaby within a lullaby, as this song tells of a widow who is singing a lullaby. Both the melody and the words carry an undertone of sorrow. When the baby grows up the mother hopes that he will go into business and sell the luxurious and dearly loved raisins and almonds.

This beautiful lullaby is probably one of the best loved and best known of the Eastern European Jewish lullabies.
Jewish

In dem bays ham - ik - dosh, In a vin _____ kl
In a room of the tem - ple, In a co - sy

chay - der zit - zt di al - mone bas Tz - iyom ale -
cor - ner There sits a wi - dow all a -

yn. Ir ben yoc - hi - dl yi - de _____ le vi - gt si
lone. With her on - ly lit - tle child which she rocks to and

k'sey - der. Un zingt im tzum shlo - fen a li - dele
fro _____ while sing - ing a love - ly lull - a -

sheyn. Un - ter Yi - dele's vi - ge - le _____ Shteyt a
by. And be - neath _ the cra - dle _____ There's a

klor____ veis tzi gele._____ Dos tz - i - gele is
lit - tle white toy *goat.* _____ *The lit - tle goat went*

ge - for - en hand - len;_____ Dos vet zein dein ber-
out a - trad - ing _____ *Just as you'll do some*

uf._____ Roz - inkes mit mand - len ____
day, _____ *Trad - ing in rai - sins and al - monds.* _

Shlof - zhe Yi - dele, shlof._____
Sleep sweet ba - by sleep. _____

Al - la al la

* In some versions, this phrase follows 'lullaby' bar 16

In dem bays hamikdosh,	*In the room of the temple, a cosy corner*
In a vinkl chayder	*There sits a widow all alone.*
Zitzt di almone bas Tziyon aleyn.	*With her only little child which she rocks to and fro*
Ir ben yochidl Yidele vigt si k'seyder.	*While singing a lovely lullaby.*
Un zingt im tzum shlofen a lidele sheyn.	*"And beneath the cradle*
Unter Yidele's vigele	*There's a little white goat,*
Shteyt a klor veis tzigele.	*The little goat went out a-trading*
Dos tzigele is geforen handlen;	*Just as you'll do some day,*
Dos vet zein dein beruf.	*Trading in raisins and almonds.*
Rozinkes mit mandlen.	*Sleep sweet baby sleep."*
Shlof-zhe Yidele, shlof.	

Other Countries

Баюшки-баю — *Russian*
Баю, баю — *Russian*
Dodo Dodo Titite — *Haitian*
Nenna Nenna — *Egyptian*

БАЮШКИ-БАЮ

SLEEP MY BABY

This lullaby is sung to a Cossack melody which is supposed to have inspired one of Russia's poets, Lerniontov, to write a poem about a soldier fighting for his country while his wife thinks of him as she rocks her baby. Some versions of this lullaby have a large number of verses. Rewards are promised to the baby but only in the form of songs and stories. *Russian*

Sleep my ba - by, sleep my dar - ling, Ba - by lul - la - by,

On your cra - dle moon is shin - ing Soft - ly from the sky.

Спи, младенецъ мой прекрасный,
   Баюшки-баю.
Тихо смотрит месяц ясный
   Въ колыбель твою.
Стану сказывать я сказки,
   Песенку спою;
Тыя дремли, закрывши глазки,
   Баюшки-баю.

Sleep my baby, sleep my darling,
Baby lullaby,
On your cradle moon is shining
Softly from the sky.

I shall sing and tell you stories,
If you close your eyes,
Slumber quietly while I lull you
Baby lullaby.

БАЮ, БАЮ

BYE YOU BYE YOU

Although this is a Russian lullaby, this version of it was collected by Kenneth Peacock in Calgary, Alberta. There are many Russian and Ukrainian families settled in western Canada and many of them still sing their original folksongs. *Russian*

Bye you,____ Bye you, bye you, shi - ki - bye you,

Go to sleep my____ glin - ka dear.____ In the

dark - est trees of the for - est, All our feath - er - ed

friends will sing,____ As they____ work to build their

nests ____ When at long last comes the ____ spring.

Баю, баю, баюшки баю,
Баю Оленьку мою.
Что на зорьке на заре,
У весенней у поре,
Птички божии поют,
В темном лесе гнезды вьют.

Баю, баю, баюшки баю,
Баю Оленьку мою.
Соловей, ты соловей,
Ты гнездо себе не вей,
Прилетай ты в наш садок,
Под веселый теремок.

Баю, баю, баюшки баю,
Баю Оленьку мою.
Кто вас детки крепко любит,
Кто вас нежно так голубит,
Не смыкая в ночи глаз,
Все заботиться о вас.

Баю, баю, баюшки баю,
Баю Оленьку мою.
Мама дорогая,
Мама золотая.
Она игрушки нам дарит,
И все сказки говорит.

Bye you, bye you, bye you, shikibye you,
Go to sleep my Glinka dear.
In the darkest trees of the forest,
All our feathered friends will sing,
As they work to build their nests
When at long last comes the Spring.

Bye you, bye you, bye you, shikibye you,
Go to sleep my Glinka dear.
Nightingale, oh nightingale,
Do not weave yourself a nest,
Fly instead to our fine orchard,
There to dwell in happiness.

Bye you, bye you, bye you, shikibye you,
Go to sleep my Glinka dear.
Who will worry about your care?
Stay awake all through the night,
Who is it that loves you dearly?
Never lets you out of her sight.

Bye you, bye you, bye you, shikibye you,
Go to sleep my Glinka dear.
It is Mother, your dear Mother,
It's your precious Mother dear,
Who'll buy toys and tell you stories,
Shelter you from harm and fear.

Dodo Dodo Titite

SLEEP, SLEEP MY LITTLE ONE

Haiti shares the island of Hispaniola with the Dominican Republic, and it is the only French speaking republic in the Western Hemisphere. Its population is largely Negro, descendants of slaves brought over from Africa. Although in their songs the African influence is noticeable because Haiti is now a tourist centre, many songs reflect European influences. Their French language is really a kind of *patois* known as Creole and it contains many Indian, African, Spanish and English words. There is much poverty, and in this lullaby the mother blames a certain general, named but unknown, for the fact that she can not give her baby any new clothes. *Haitian*

Do do do do titi - te,___ Do - do sou bras man - man.___ Gen-er-
Sleep, sleep my lit - tle one___ Sleep, sleep in moth - er's arms.___ Gen-er-

al La - car - os rété Anse à Veau Pas quit - té anyien___ pou titite à moin.
al La - car - os in Anse à Veau Didn't leave any - thing for my child.

M'ob - li - ge coupé___ jup - on moin P'oum fait cas - que pou' titite à moin.
I have cut up my un - der skirt To make dress - es for my child.

Dodo dodo titite,
Dodo sou bras manman.
General Lacaros rété Anse à Veau
Pas quitté anyien pou titite à moin.

M'oblige coupé jupon moin
Pou'm fait casque pou' titite à moin.

Sleep, sleep my little one,
Sleep, sleep in mother's arms
General Lacaros in Anse à Veau
Didn't leave anything for my child.

I have cut up my underskirt
To make dresses for you my child.

Nenna Nenna

SLUMBER SONG

This song, collected by Baheega Sidky Rasheed, was one of many heard in her childhood and written down for her own pleasure, and in order to preserve it. Her translation is intended to present the idea of the song rather than its literal meaning word by word. In order to sing these words in English they have to be adapted to fit this highly ornate melody. An adaptation has been suggested for the first verse and the refrain. *Egyptian*

Nen - na, nen - na, nen - na ho, Nen - na nen - na nam nen -
Sleep my ba - by, close thine eyes,___ Sleep my ba - by sleep thee

na. Dee hâ - bee - ba wa - na___ wa ĥ - i - b - ba -
well. My own A - dored, I ev - en love___ all___ those that love___

ha ___ Wa ĥib - ba - nal lee ___ yi - ĥib - ba - ha.
thee, ___ I love the rose, be - cause thy___ cheeks are of its hue. ___

There are many more verses in Egyptian, and here are three more translated into English, which, following the pattern of the one under the music, can be fitted to the music, remembering that the refrain is sung at the beginning of each verse.

REFRAIN:

Nen-na, nen-na, nen-na ho
Nen-na, nen-na, nam ņen-na.
Dee ĥa-bee-ba wa-na ĥib-ba-ha
Wa-ĥib-ba-nal-lee yi-ĥib-ba-ha.

REFRAIN:
Sleep my baby, close thine eyes,
Sleep my baby, sleep thee well.
My own Adored,
I even love all those that love thee,
I love the rose,
Because thy cheeks are of its hue.

God bless you dear in slumber sweet,
Those pigeons two your meal will be.
O do not fear the gentle pair,
Ne'er will I harm the pigeons fair.

Sleep baby mine, God watches near,
Two crickets small I'll bring to you.
O fear no harm, you crickets small,
My baby sleeps, as you sing near.

O dear beloved, my own sweet child
Ne'er will I let you wander far,
And when you marry I'll be near,
For life without you holds no joy.

Sources and Acknowledgements

Below are given references to printed or recorded sources of the songs. Many of the songs appear in other books and records than those listed, but as far as possible the references given are to the earliest or the most complete source. For some of the lullabies the author has drawn upon the common heritage, as she remembers them, from her mother, and the version given may not be identical with source material.

The authors' thanks are due to the collectors, authors and publishers who have given us permission to use copyright material. They are listed individually, in the list of sources which follows.

Thanks for the use of records and information about records is due to Folkways Ethnic Library, New York, The Record Centre, Montreal, and Sam and Lee Gesser of Montreal.

For the use of twelve lullabies transcribed from a Folkways recording, "Lullabies of the World," special thanks are due to the collector, Lillian Mendelssohn. The songs are listed as in the index, except where there are titles, when these are used instead of first lines.

CANADA

BA BA BABY, Collected by Dr. Helen Creighton, *Maritime Folk Songs*, Ryerson Press Ltd., Toronto, Ontario, 1956.

DORS DORS LE P'TIT BIBI, Collected by Dr. Helen Creighton, *Folk Music From Nova Scotia*, Folkways Ethnic Lib. F.W. 4006, New York, 1956.

TAH NE BAH, Collected by Barbara Cass-Beggs from Dorothy Francis of Regina, Saskatchewan, *Eight Songs of Saskatchewan*, Canadian Music Sales Corp. Ltd., Toronto, Ontario, 1965 and *Folk Songs of Saskatchewan*, Folkways Ethnic Lib. F.E. 4312, New York, 1963.

BÍ BÍ OG BLAKA, *Hörpuhl Jömar, Islenzk Songlög*, Fjórar Karlmannar and Sigfús Einarsson, Reykjavik, 1905, Dept. of Icelandic Literature, University of Manitoba, Winnipeg, Manitoba.

STILL NOW AND HEAR MY SINGING, Collected by Dr. Richard Johnston from the Rev. D. H. Whitbread, *Folk Songs Of Canada*, Edith Fowke and Richard Johnston, Waterloo Music Co., Waterloo, Ontario, 1954.

C'EST LA POULETTE GRISE, *French Songs for Children*, Alan Mills, Folkways F.C. 7208 (F.P. 708 F.C. 7018), New York, 1953.

HO HO WATENAY, Collected by Alan Mills, *Canada's Story In Song*, Edith Fowke, Alan Mills, Helmut Blume, W. J. Gage Ltd., Scarborough, Ontario, 1960.

UNITED STATES

ALL THE PRETTY LITTLE HORSES, Collected by Moe Asch, *Lullabies and Rounds*, Folkways Album No. 601, New York.

O MOTHER GLASCO, *American Negro Songs*, Crown Publications Inc., New York.

MARY HAD A BABY, *A Christmas Festival Pageant*, Barbara Cass-Beggs, Waterloo Music Co., Waterloo, Ontario, 1964.

BYE BYE BABY, Collected by Cecil J. Sharp, *English Folk Songs of the Southern Appalachians*, Edited by Maud Karpeles, Oxford University Press, Toronto, Canada. 1st Ed. 1932, 2nd Ed. 1952 (London/New York).

THE MOCKING BIRD, Collected by Moe Asch, Cub. No. 1 (Adeline Van Wey), New York.

BRITISH ISLES

THE WEE LITTLE CROODIN DOO, Collected by Lucy Broadwood, *Journal Of The English Folk Song Society*, Vol. 5 of 8 Vols., London, 1899-1928.

DANCE A BABY DIDDY, As sung by Mrs. C. E. M. Cass. Can be found in *The Baby's Opera*, Walter Crane, Frederick Warne and Co. Ltd., London and New York.

DANCE TO YOUR DADDY, Collected by Cecil J. Sharp, *A Selection of Folk Songs Vol. 2*, Cecil J. Sharp and Ralph Vaughan Williams, Novello and Co. Ltd., London, 1908-1912.

NEWCASTLE LULLABY, Collected by A. Gilchrist, *Journal Of The English Folk Song Society*, Vol. 5 of 8 Vols., London, 1899-1928.

SUO-GÂN, Collected by W. S. Gwynn Williams, *Old Welsh Folk Songs*, J. Curwen and Sons Ltd., London, 1927.

CROON, Collected by A. Gilchrist, *Journal Of The English Folk Song Society*, Vol. 5 of 8 Vols., London, 1899-1928.

CAN YE SEW CUSHIONS, *The Scots Musical Museum*, James Johnson, Vol. 5 of 6 Volumes of Scotch Folk Songs, Edinburgh, 1787-1803. Edinburgh and London. 3rd Ed. 1853.

KISHMUL CRADLE CROON, Collected by Marjorie Kennedy Fraser and Kenneth Macleod, *Songs Of The Hebrides Vol. 2*, Boosey and Hawkes Inc., London and New York, 1917.

HÒ HO BHO LAIDI BHEAG, Collected by Polly Hitchcock, *Songs And Pipes Of The Hebrides*, Folkways Ethnic Lib. F. E. 4430, New York, 1952.

CODAIL A LEANB, Collected by Herbert Hughes, *Irish Country Songs Vol. 1*, Boosey and Hawkes Inc., London and New York, 1909.

USHAG VEG RUY, Collected by A. W. Moore, *Twelve Manx Folk Songs Vol. 1*, Arnold Foster and Mona Douglas, Stainer and Bell Ltd., Reigate, Surrey, England.

I'VE FOUND MY BONNY BABE A NEST, Collected by George Petrie, *The Complete Collection Of Irish Music*, Charles Villiers Stanford, Boosey and Hawkes Inc., London and New York, 1905.

HUSH-A-BYE BABY, ON THE TREE TOP, As sung by Mrs. C. E. M. Cass. Can be found in *The Baby's Opera*, Walter Crane, Frederick Warner and Co. Ltd., London and New York.

SCANDINAVIA AND NORTHWESTERN EUROPE

NAA SKA'EN LITEN FAA SOVA SOA SÖDT, Collected by Engel Lund, *Second Book Of Folksongs*, Oxford University Press, London, New York, Toronto, 1949.

RO RO RELTE, *Folk Songs Of Europe*, Dr. Maud Karpeles, Novello and Co., London, 1956.

HIST HYOR VEJEN SLÄR EN BUGT, *Danish Folksongs*, Inger Nielson, Folkways F. W. 8819, New York, 1965.

VYSSA LULLA LITET BARN, *Folk Songs Of Europe*, Dr. Maud Karpeles, Novello and Co., London, 1956, Oak Publications, New York, 1956.

MANA GALLAKA NOUKAT, Collected by Wolfgang Laade and Dieter Christensen, *Lappish Joik Songs From Northern Norway*, Folkways Ethnic Lib. P1007, New York, 1956.

SOFDU ÚNGA ÁSTIN MÍN, Collected by S. V. Sveinbjornsson, *Islenzk Bjodlog*, R. W. Pentland, Edinburgh, 1933.

KEHTO LAULA, Collected by John A. Stark, *Tunes And Songs Of Finland*, Folkways F. W. 6856, New York, 1957.

WESTERN AND SOUTHERN EUROPE

SCHLAF, KINDLEIN SCHLAF, Volks-Kinderliedes. Johanne Brahms. Arranged and published 1858. Dedicated to the Schumann children. *Children's Folk Songs Of Germany*, Folkways F.C. 7742, New York, 1960.

SCHLAF, IN GUTER RUH, *Lullabies Of The World*, Lillian Mendelssohn, Folkways Ethnic Lib. F.E. 4511, New York, 1964.

DO DO KINDJE VAN DE MINNE, Collected by Van Duyse, *Komt Vriewden Come Friends*, Co-operative Recreation Services Inc., R. 1, Delaware, Ohio, U.S.A., 1961.

HOE LAAT IS'T?, Collected by Jaap Kunst, *Living Folksongs And Dance Tunes From The Netherlands*, Folkways F.P. 70/1, New York, 1956.

FAIS DODO, *Favourite French Folk Songs*, Alan Mills, Oak Publications, New York, 1963.

FAIS DODO LOLA MABELLE, *Lullabies Of The World*, Lillian Mendelssohn, Folkways Ethnic Lib. F. E. 4511, New York, 1964.

A LA NANITA NANA, Collected by Eleanor Paz, *Favourite Spanish Folk Songs*, Oak Publications, New York, 1956.

DODO, L'ENFANT DORS, *Lullabies Of The World*, Lillian Mendelssohn, Folkways Ethnic Lib. F. E. 4511, New York, 1964.

NÂNEZ BINAMÊYE POYÈTE, *Lullabies Of The World*, Lillian Mendelssohn, Folkways Ethnic Lib. F.E. 4511, New York, 1964.

FI LA NANAE, MI BEL FIOLE, *Folk Songs Of Europe*, Dr. Maud Karpeles, Novello and Co., London, 1956, Oak Publications, New York, 1956.

RÓ RÓ, Collected by Kurt Schindler, *Anthology Of Portuguese Music*, Vol. 1 Trasosmontes, Folkways Ethnic Lib. F.E. 4538, New York, 1962.

KORMATAI TO MOROUTZKO MOU, *Folk Songs Of Europe*, Dr. Maud Karpeles, Novello and Co., London, 1956, Oak Publications, New York, 1956.

ELA YPNE, Sung to author by Evangelia Paraskevopoulos who learnt it from her mother, Lilika Dimitriadov (Sparta, Asia. Minor).

NAM, NAM, Collected by George Bonavia, *Folk Songs And Music From Malta*, Folkways F. M. 4047, New York, 1964.

CENTRAL AND EASTERN EUROPE

AIJA ANZIT AIJA, *Lullabies Of The World*, Lillian Mendelssohn, Folkways Ethnic Lib. F. E. 4511, New York, 1964.

MOČIUTE MANO, *Lullabies Of The World*, Lillian Mendelssohn, Folkways Ethnic Lib. F. E. 4511, New York, 1964.

HEJ PADA PADA ROSIÇKA, Sung to author by Anne Hruchair of Ottawa. Can also be found in *Folk Songs And Footnotes*, World Publications Co., Cleveland, New York, 1960, 5th Pub. 1964.

ALUDJ BABA ALUDJÁL, *Lullabies Of The World*, Lillian Mendelssohn, Folkways Ethnic Lib. F. E. 4511, New York, 1964.

USNIJ, USNIJ, *Lullabies Of The World*, Lillian Mendelssohn, Folkways Ethnic Lib. F.E. 4511, New York, 1964.

LATIN AMERICA

DUÉRMETE MI NIÑO, *Lullabies Of The World*, Lillian Mendelssohn, Folkways Ethnic Lib. F.E. 4511, New York, 1964.

A LA RORRO NIÑO, *Lullabies Of The World*, Lillian Mendelssohn, Folkways Ethnic Lib. F.E. 4511, New York, 1964.

DORMITE NIÑITO, Collected by Jim Morse, *Folk Songs Of The Caribbean*, Bantam Books, New York, 1958.

DORMITE NIÑITO, *Songs And Dances Of Honduras*, Folkways 10 384, New York.

DUÉRMETE NIÑO CHIQUITO, *Lullabies Of The World*, Lillian Mendelssohn, Folkways Ethnic Lib. F.E. 4511, New York, 1964.

DUERME NIÑO PEQUEÑITO, *Lullabies Of The World*, Lillian Mendelssohn, Folkways Ethnic Lib. F.E. 4511, New York, 1964.

ROUXINOL DO PICO PRETO, *Lullabies Of The World*, Lillian Mendelssohn, Folkways Ethnic Lib. F.E. 4511, New York, 1964.

ARRORO MI NIÑO, *Lullabies Of The World*, Lillian Mendelssohn, Folkways Ethnic Lib. F.E. 4511, New York, 1964.

AFRICA

SLEEP MY BABY, *Follow The Sunset*, Charity Bailey and Robert Emmett, Folkways F.C. 7406, New York, 1953.

YEKE OMO MI, *Hi Neighbour Series No. 3*, United States Committee for U.N.I.C.E.F.

CONGO LULLABY, *The Whole World Singing*, Edith Lovell Thomas, Friendship Press, New York, 1950.

ASIA

HAWA DHERAY AANA, Collected from Mrs. Kailash Anand, Montreal, P.Q., 1966. Also available on Angel Record 45/New Delhi, India 7TJE-548.

NINNI BABA, Indian Co-operative Recreation Service Inc., R. 1, Delaware, Ohio, U.S.A., 1956.

THE BAMBOO FLUTE, *Follow The Sunset*, Charity Bailey and Robert Emmett, Folkways F.C. 7460, New York, 1953.

THREE SINHALESE LULLABIES, The Hon. L.S.B. Perera, High Commissioner for Ceylon, Ottawa, Ontario, on behalf of the Government of Ceylon.

SLUMBER SONG, Collected by Saranagupta Amarsinha, *Sinhalese Folk Songs*, Colombo, Ceylon.

KOMORIUTA, *Japanese Children's Songs*, Shugi Tsugawo, Fuji Publishing Co. Ltd., Tokyo, Japan, 1959.

LULLABY, Collected from *United Nations Songs of The People*, by Henry Cowell, With permission from S.C. Schirmer Inc. New York.

JEWISH

LULLA LULLA LULLABY, Collected by Miriam Ben-Ezra, *Israeli Songs For Children*, Folkways F.C. 7226, New York, 1958.

AYLE LYULE, Collected by Ruth Rubin, *Jewish Folk Songs*, Oak Publications, New York, 1965.

ZOLST AZOY LEBN UN ZAYN GEZINT, Collected by Ruth Rubin, *Jewish Folk Songs*, Oak Publications, New York, 1965.

ROZINKES MIT MANDLEN, Collected by Abraham Goldfadden. Recorded and translated by Alan Mille on *Raasche and Alan Mills Sing Jewish Folksongs* 1962 Folkways F W 8711. With permission from Alan Mills and Folkways.

OTHER COUNTRIES

SLEEP MY BABY, Sung to author, and also found in: *Songs Of The Russian People*, C. Shvedoll and Tatiana Smirnova, Federated Russian Orthodox Clubs, New York, 1939.

BAIO, BAIO, Collected by Kenneth Peacock, *Kenneth Peacock Collection*, National Museum of Canada, Ottawa, 1967.

DODO DODO TITITE, Collected by Frantz Casseus, *Haitian Folk Songs*, Lolita Cuevas and Frantz Casseus, Folkways F.P. 811, New York, 1953.

NENNA NENNA, Collected by Baheega Sidky Rasheed, *Egyptian Folk Songs*, Oak Publications, New York, 1965.

BIBLIOGRAPHY

List of Publications consulted in addition to books mentioned under the section Sources of Songs.

Botsford, Florence Hudson, *Folksongs of Many People, Vol. 1*, Women's Press, New York, 1921.

Chase, Gilbert, *Latin American Folk Music*, Lib. of Congress; *Bibliography of Latin American Folk Music*, Washington, 1942.

Chase, Gilbert, *America's Music*, McGraw Hill Book Co., Inc., New York, London, Toronto, 1955.

Daiken, Leslie, *The Lullaby Book*, Edmund Ward Ltd., London, 1959.

Driver, Harold E., *Indians of North America*, University of Chicago Press, Chicago, U.S.A.; Toronto University Press, Toronto, Ontario, Canada, 1961.

Dunstan, R. and Bygott, C. E., *Musical Appreciation Through Song*, Schofield and Sims Ltd., Huddersfield, York, England, 1933.

Grove , Sir George, *Dictionary of Music and Musicians*, Eric Blom Fifth Edition, Vol. 3, Macmillan and Co., London, 1945.

Mason, Redfern, *The Songlore of Ireland*, Wessels and Bissel and Co., London, 1910; Baker and Taylor Co., New York, 1911.

Nelte, Bruno, *Music in Primitive Culture*, Cambridge Harvard University Press, 1956.

Newmarsh, Rosa, *The Music of Czechoslovakia*, Oxford University Press, London, New York, Toronto, 1942.

Opie, Iona and Peter, *The Oxford Nursery Rhyme Book*, Oxford University Press, London, New York, Toronto, 1955, 1957.

Opie, Iona and Peter. *The Oxford Dictionary of Nursery Rhymes*, Oxford University Press, London, New York, Toronto, 1951, 1955.

Phillips, William J., *Carols, Their Origin, Music and Connection With Mystery Plays*, George Routledge and Sons, Ltd., London; E. P. Dutton and Co., New York, 1921.

Sandburg, Carl, *The American Songbag*, Harcourt, Brace and Co., New York, 1927.

Sharp, Cecil J., *English Folk Carols*, Wessex Press, Taunton, Somerset, England; Novello and Co., London, 1911.

Sharp, Cecil J., *English Folksong*, Methuen and Co. Ltd., London, 1907, 1936, 1954.

Slonimsky, Nicolas, *Music of Latin America*, Thomas Y. Crowell and Co., New York, 1945.

Stanford, Villiers Charles and Forsyth, C., *A History of Music*, Macmillan and Co., London, 1925.

Stevens, Dennis, *A History of Song*, Hutchinson and Co., London, 1960; W. W. Norton and Co., New York, 1961.

White, Newman I., *American Negro Folk Songs*, Cambridge Harvard University Press, 1928.

Wissler, Clark, *North American Indians of The Plains*, American Museum of Natural History, New York, 1934.